JESUS WOULD HAVE BEEN A SCRATCH GOLFER

By Chuck Hammett

Foreword by Kenny Knox

Jesus Would Have Been A Scratch Golfer

Copyright © 1995 by Cross Training Publishing

Library of Congress Cataloging-in-Publication Data

ISBN 1-887002-23-5
Hammett, Chuck
Chuck Hammett

Jesus Would Have Been A Scratch Golfer / Chuck Hammett
Published by Cross Training Publishing, Grand Island, Nebraska
68803

Distributed in the United States and Canada by Cross Training
Publishing

Sketches: Tracy Daughtry
Cover illustrator: Jeff Sharpton
Photography: Larry Coltharp & Greg Furr
Printed in the United States of America

For additional books and resources available
through Cross Training Publishing contact us at:

Cross Training Publishing
P.O. Box 1541
Grand Island, NE 68802
(308) 384-5762

Dedication

I would like to dedicate this book to the Lord. May it bring a smile to your face and glorify Your kingdom. I look forward to the day when I get to go Home and be with You forever. (**1 Thessalonians 4:17**)

About the Cover

The cover uses the twelfth (12th) hole at Augusta National Golf Course as its background setting. This hole is included in the stretch of holes famously known as "Amen Corner." This spiritual reference reminds us of the necessity to give ourselves continually to prayer and the ministry of the Word. (Acts 6:4)

Finally, the flag on the green has been replaced with an illuminated cross. This is to show us what we are ultimately shooting for, and that our aim in life is to be transformed by the resurrection power given after His death on the cross. (See Philippians 3:10-14)

Acknowledgements:

The writing and publication of this book has been very enjoyable. The long hours have been well worth the wait to have the final product. However, I cannot take all of the credit for myself. There are many people I want to thank for helping make this book a reality:

Family: I want to thank my parents, Richard and Lynn, and my brother, Trey for giving me support and believing in me throughout this entire endeavor.

Prayer Group: thanks to Tige, Ross, Tom, and Rick for the continual prayer support and love you have shown me over the last two years. You have all helped me grow in the Lord and to see this project through.

First Baptist Tallahassee: for all of your prayer support and encouragement.

Jim Duval: for rooting me in solid golf mechanics, helping me to be a better teacher, and and all of your personal attention to my game from early days.

Dave Fiori: for your professional touch to the editing of the manuscript, while being sensitive to the spiritual meaning and flavor of the book.

Judy Leckey: for being so patient and easy to work with while typesetting the book, and working extra hours to meet our deadline.

Nick Davis, Michelle Donkin, and **Robert Baggs:** for making the fundraising end of this book a personal priority. Without your help and commitment, this book would not be a reality.

Kenny and Karen Knox: for being good friends, and going well out of your way to be a part of this ministry. Your commitment to the Lord shines through in all that you do.

Holy Spirit: for guiding and directing me when feeling like I had nowhere to go.

Lord Jesus: for being my Lord and Savior, and always being by my side. **Almighty God:** for giving me the vision to write this book for You. and showing me the direction to take this book and ministry. All glory to You!

Foreword

by Kenny Knox

"Be anxious for nothing, but in everything by prayer and supplication, with thanksgiving, let your requests be made known to God". **(Phillippians 4:6)** I know in my heart that God has a plan for each and every one of us.

When I decided to open a golf academy in Tallahassee back in April of 1994, I did not know how the Lord was going to use me through it. I did know that I wanted to put something back into the game that had been so good to me. I wanted to provide a service to the community that had supported me over the years. My burning desire to introduce young people to the game that has been such an important part of my life, was also a major factor. However, I realized these were simply my own personal desires. Thankfully, through prayer and seeking God's will, the Lord has changed my outlook on personal desires. These desires are now to further the kingdom of God.

In looking back, furthering the kingdom of God has not always been a top priority. I grew up going to church in Columbus, Georgia. The problem is that I was going to be around my friends, not to have a relationship with God. From a very young age, I had decided golf would be my god. The more I played and the better I got, the less time I spent in church. From a golfing perspective, my career started developing nicely. I won the state high school championships in Georgia as a sophomore. I received a scholarship to play at Florida State University where I earned all-American honors. I started my professional career strong by winning the first mini-tour event I entered. There was nothing to stop me. In 1982, I reached the highest level of competition by qualifying for the P.G.A. tour. In my mind I thought this was it; I had finally made it. There would be no more worries in life. This mentality soon changed.

In my first year on tour, I earned less than $7,000. The struggle to survive on tour was great, and I did not have a source of strength to turn to. All of this changed for me in 1984 when I married my wife, Karen. Her strong influence showed me what living a Christian life was all about, and that having a relationship with God was much more important than worshiping the game of golf. I accepted Jesus Christ as my personal Lord and Savior that year, and all aspects of my life changed for the better. Through God's grace, I have been able to win three times on tour and have a very successful career.

I received a phone call one day from a young man named Chuck Hammett. He told me the Lord had led him to write a book sharing ministry through golf instruction, and wanted to know if I would consider the possibility of getting involved in the project. I made arrangements for Chuck to come to my house to discuss the book and my involvement. In discussing the book and golf mechanics, we soon discovered our paths had crossed before in sharing the same teacher, Jim Duval. Jim had been the head professional at my home club in Tallahassee before moving to Chuck's club in Venice, Fla. It may seem like a coincidence, yet I believe it was a bond orchestrated by the Lord.

It did not take long before Chuck and I became friends. Chuck impressed me so much with his knowledge of the golf swing, that I offered him a position as instructor at my golf academy. More importantly, he impressed me as a person. A true brother in Christ. Someone who is truly dedicated to our Lord and Saviour, Jesus Christ. Wanting to get involved in this book was an easy decision. It was easy to see that "Jesus Would Have Been A Scratch Golfer" is about furthering the kingdom of God. I am just glad to know that this objective continues to be top priority in my life.

God Bless You,

Kenny Knox

Table of Contents

Introduction

"In the beginning God created the heavens and earth." **(Gen. 1:1)** The latter of the two is truly an amazing creation, and I look forward to seeing the first someday.

As I was sitting on the back porch this morning, I was simply admiring God's creation and observing its magnificence. The wind was gently pushing back the branches of the palm trees as they kept watch over the bay's calm waters. The pelicans were taking turns "dive-bombing" for the catch of the day, as the fish rushed for protection under the limbs of the mangroves. The warmth of the sun felt good on my back as I was prayerfully preparing for another day. The hustle and bustle of activities reminded me of the instruments in an orchestra coming together in harmony at just the right moment. Surrounding all of this was the powerful blue sky, keeping its watch on the orchestra with the eyes of a conductor.

I am always awestruck when I stop long enough to observe the magnitude and power of the Lord's creation. I so often take for granted the beauty Dad provides us in His creation. Truly, it is magnificent.

This observation of God's work was achieved by simply turning my head a few degrees on the back porch of my parent's house. There is also another place where the awareness of God's creation always creeps into the front of my mind. This may sound peculiar, but I find spiritual peace on the golf course.

I know that God created the heavens and earth in the first six days and rested on the seventh, but I think there is an outside chance that on the eighth day God took out his paint brushes and created golf courses. He must have let his imagination run wild, smiling the whole time he was at work.

I can just see God having a good time by grabbing a stroke of blue and adding more water at Pebble Beach, then digging Royal St. George's bunkers a little deeper with a dab of white, and making the greens at Augusta ever so slick with some fine green shavings. (I bet He used a thin brush for that one.)

There is an observation about the game of golf that states, "Golf will take you to some of the most beautiful places on earth." I agree and would also add that it has some of the most spiritual.

There is no doubt about it, we cannot escape God's creation on a golf course. The grass, trees, sand, water, wind, and sky are everywhere. Of course, some of us are more prone to finding these hazards than others.

I have been stepping into this golfing realm of creation since I was 7 years old and am very thankful for all the fun times, challenges, memories, opportunities, and friendships it has brought to me. I also look forward to the memories and lessons that are in store for me. The Lord has certainly been good to me through this wonderful game.

It is my intention in writing this book to share with you my knowledge of golf and my passion for the Lord in a way that you have never thought of. I do not claim to be a Bible scholar or preacher, yet I do know Jesus Christ as my savior and the Lord as the focal point of my life. I also believe there are many aspects of God's love that need to be shared. I have a great enthusiasm for teaching others the fundamentals of the golf swing, and I want to share some of God's love with you through my teaching.

So, I hope you are excited about learning some new ways to improve your golf swing and to look at your relationship with the Lord in a way that will cause it to be enhanced and set on fire. I invite you to come aboard as one of my personal students and to get ready for a thrilling ride.

South-Paw Note

I want to apologize to all of the left-handed golfers out there who have had to mirror the instruction for the right-handed golfers. I hope it is not too difficult to apply all of the teachings to your golf swing. Out of respect, I dedicate this whole page to you.

Getting Started

It is always interesting for me to go out to the driving range and simply watch others hit golf balls. I can almost always predict how the beginner or inexperienced amateur will begin their practice session: They reach into their bag for the driver. The new golfer, before having had any instruction or putting any mental effort into the mechanics of the golf swing, simply wants to see how far he can hit the ball. I guess everybody wants to swing the driver hard and be the next John Daly.

I can understand this type of enthusiasm, but it is probably doing more harm than good. Think of all the bad habits you are learning by using the "grip it and rip it" mentality. I firmly believe that if a new golfer will exercise some patience and discipline in his approach to the game, his future in golf will be much happier.

The idea of getting started with the simple, yet important, aspects of the game reminds me of when I started reading the Bible for the first time. I wanted to read about Jesus, but I did not ask anyone the best place to start. I was about 13 years old, and I decided I could figure it out. I opened my Bible to page one and the book of Genesis. I got through the creation of the world and man, the Garden of Eden and the serpent, and even the accounts of Noah and the ark. I then ran into a big stumbling block with the listing of all the names in Japeth's family. There was a lot of begotting going on, and my attention span was short. I was only on page 13, realized there were about a thousand more pages to go, and I had not read the name of Jesus once. My effort to read the Bible fell short rather quickly. I would bet a lot of new Christians have done the same thing.

My point is that I did not know where to start. If I had been directed to the book of John, where all the red ink can be found, I probably would have read longer than 20 minutes. I think the same can be said for the beginning golfer. If the basics can be mastered first, he will probably stay on the driving range longer than 20 minutes and may even want to go back for more. With this in mind, I think it is necessary to start your instruction by mastering one of the most simple and important aspects of the game: the grip.

THE GRIP:

If we are going to learn how to play this magnificent game using these funny-looking sticks, don't you think it would be smart to learn how to properly hold on to them? A good grip will lead to many positive results throughout the swing.

Let us first start by looking at the positioning of the left hand on the club. When placing the club in the palm of your hand, it is very important to have the shaft resting underneath what is called the hypothenar muscle. This is the padding at the bottom of your hand in line with your pinky finger. The shaft, when resting underneath this muscle and in the middle joint of your forefinger, will lie at a 45-degree angle. This provides great support of the club which can be held in this position with minimal effort. Try this yourself. You will find that you can hold the club like this very easily. From here, simply allow your last three fingers to wrap around the end of the club. You are now in position to place your thumb straight down the shaft at 12:00, or slightly to the right at 1:00. Either one is acceptable as long as you do not turn your hand too far to the right.

Having established a solid left-hand grip, let's look at the right hand. Envision the palm of your right hand as a pocket. When placing your right hand on the club, think of the thumb of your left hand fitting into the middle of this pocket. It is like your left thumb is being swallowed. Disregarding your right pinky finger for now, let the three middle fingers of your right hand naturally wrap around the shaft. From here you can let your right thumb rest on the club slightly left of center at approximately 11:00.

Now we come to the personalized part of the grip. This involves the way you place the right pinky finger on the club. There are three traditional choices.

Grip # 1: Overlapping

This method allows you to place your right pinky in between and on top of the forefinger and middle finger of your left hand. The pinky finger rests on top of the other two. I would recommend this grip to those of with medium or large hands.

Grip # 2: Interlocking

In this case, the left forefinger will release itself from inside the "pocket" and lock together with the right pinky. The left forefinger is now resting on the back side of the right hand. I would recommend this grip for someone with slightly smaller hands. This should give you a little more strength.

Grip # 3: Ten Fingered

This grip is also called the baseball grip. Here, the right pinky wraps around the shaft with the other three fingers of the right hand. This is very similar to the way you would hold a baseball bat. This grip is not as commonly used as the other two, yet it can be very effective depending upon your preference. I had a good friend growing up who used this grip and played very well, so do not be afraid to use it if it is comfortable.

[Note: If you are not sure which of the three grips to use, practice some shots using all three, and go with the one that is the most comfortable.]

Trigger Finger:

There is one more important aspect in the positioning of the right hand. It is natural to have a slight gap between the right forefinger and middle finger, and that is good. It might resemble the feeling of pulling a trigger on a gun. This "triggering" position allows you to sense the weight of the club going to the top of your swing and through impact. These points will be discussed later. So, if you have your right forefinger crammed in tight to the middle finger, relax it, and put a little breathing space in between.

The Two V's:

Finally, notice the "V" shape formed between the thumb and forefinger of each hand. The direction these two "V"s point can help you know if your hands are on the club properly. A good check point is to make sure

8

the "V" from your right hand points to just inside your right shoulder, and the "V" on your left hand points to about three inches to the left on the hump of your collar bone. You can check this by extending two lines from your hands up to your shoulder. This is simple, yet effective. Remember to check your "V"s.

Praise the Lord! The positioning of the hands is one of the hardest things to master, and you are well on your way to conquering this task. However, because of its importance, you should get in the habit of checking your grip on a regular basis. We are not, however, finished with the grip. There is one aspect of the grip I want you to consider with the utmost respect: grip pressure.

Grip Pressure:

Students, please treat this part of the grip with great reverence. It is a key that can save you strokes immediately. I rank grip pressure as one of the most important parts of the golf swing.

In looking at your left hand, the pressure points are found in your last three fingers. On your right hand, the pressure points are found in the middle and ring fingers. It is good to know where the pressure points are, but the most important thing to remember is just how much pressure to apply.

I think the pioneers of this game made a great mistake by naming the end of the club the grip. When I traditionally think of the word grip, I think of a vice clamping onto something with a lot of strength. The dictionary actually defines the word grip as, "the power of grasping firmly." These words have tightness and tension written all over them.

I want you to try something taking a golf club and applying your newly learned grip. Now, hold the club with as much pressure in your hands and forearms as you can muster, and try to make a smooth golf swing. It is virtually impossible. So why do most of us have a strangle hold on the club when we take our grip? We may not be playing the kind of golf we want to, but this is no reason to take it out on the handle of the club.

If I would have been a founding father of this game, I would have fought to the death in making sure the end of the club was named the "soft." This just sounds so much nicer. If you can remain soft in your "soft", it will relax your hands, arms, shoulders, and allow your muscles to move the way God designed them to.

If we are going to make a smooth, flowing golf swing, doesn't it make sense to keep our muscles soft and relaxed? A good teaching friend of mine, Becky Sauers, insists that you need to feel like you are holding a tube of toothpaste in your hands with the cap off without allowing any paste to come out. (Don't worry, my father is a dentist, and we can replace your tube if you try this at home and splatter toothpaste all over your bathroom mirror.) You will be amazed at how lightly you can hold on to a golf club and never lose control of it throughout your swing. In the 18 years I have been playing golf, I have never seen a club come flying out of someone's hands.

The bottom line is that many golfers hold the club too tight. You can practically see the blood flowing through their bulging veins. When working on my own grip pressure, I have a tip which often helps me. I like to think of the grip/soft as the world we live in. It is so easy for people, including myself, to cling tightly to the things of this world for security and self-assurance. People hold on to money, material things, drugs, sex, people, status, and the list goes on and on.

Have you ever seen the poster of the cat at the end of a rope with the caption reading, "Hold on tight?" I sometimes think we get to the end of our "wordly" ropes and hold on with all our might. However, the Lord is calling us to just let go. If we can let go of the end of the "wordly" rope and fall into the loving arms of Jesus, the security and self-assurance we are looking for will immediately come into view. The Lord looks after his children. This world is presently dominated by Satan, but if we let go of the world, Jesus Christ will lead us down a road of victory to His kingdom. I know this is a victorious road because I cheated and looked in the back of the book at Revelation. **WE WIN!**

I know letting go of the worldly rope is not easy to do, but the Lord will give you a comfortable landing by trusting in Him. **Proverbs 3:5 & 6** states, *"Trust in the Lord with all your heart, and lean not on your own understanding; In all your ways acknowledge Him, and He will make straight your paths."*

When working on your grip pressure, let go of all that tension and tightness. If you will trust in a soft grip the way Solomon teaches us to trust in the Lord in Proverbs, your golf shots just might be made straight as well. Give them both a try; I know you will like the results.

Set-Up

The next area I want to focus on is the set-up or address. I know that we have yet to hit a ball, but I cannot overemphasize the importance of your preswing mechanics. I mentioned before that if we cannot hold on to the club properly, it will be very difficult to make a good golf swing. It should also make sense that we need to properly position our body while standing over the ball if we expect to make a good golf swing.

Before proceeding with the description of the set-up, I want to define the term square. The term refers to being in line with, or coming into conformity with, your desired target line or swing plane. The set-up that will be described from this point on will be in reference to your body line. The target line and swing plane will be discussed thoroughly in coming sections. Keep this definition of "square" fresh in your mind as we continue.

The Feet:

We might as well start from the ground up, so let's first look at our feet in the set-up. We want our feet to be aligned in a square position which places our feet parallel to our "target line" as opposed to being on an open or closed line to our target. A good reminder for how far apart to keep our feet is the width of our shoulders. However, I would suggest that you not take a stance much wider than this, because as it becomes wider, it becomes more difficult to turn your hips and shoulders.

Make the comparison on your own. First, stand with your feet completely together and notice the ease with which you can turn your body. Next, take a very wide stance, and you will see that your turning motion encounters a much greater resistance. This comparison can also be seen in spinning a rock on the end of a rope. A tighter rotation spins faster and easier.

Finally, I want you to turn your left foot slightly open to the left. This does not mean pulling your foot back off of your square plane, but simply rotating it open about 25 degrees. This will allow your body to turn toward the finish more easily. Perhaps you have heard the term, "clearing your hips." By opening your left foot, you are in a better position to clear your hips or turn them completely toward the target.

Our feet are obviously what we build the foundation of our golf swing upon, but what is the best way to build a foundation for our lives?

Paul reveals to us in **I Corinthians 3:10, 11** that, *"According to the grace of God which was given to me, as a wise master builder I have laid the foundation, and another builds on it. But let each one take heed how he builds on it. For no other foundation can anyone lay than that which is laid, which is Jesus Christ."*

Wow, this is truly a powerful statement. The foundation of Jesus Christ will certainly provide the strength and support you need to face the trials and tribulations of life. I hope that when you take your stance on the golf course, you will not only remember the principles of building a solid physical foundation, but also the solid rock of Jesus Christ upon which to build the foundation of your life. **(See Matt. 7:24-25)**

Posture:

Now that we have established a good foundation, let's build upon it by developing correct posture. At this point, I want you to simply stand straight up. Go ahead, get up out of your chair and stand up. This is your lesson, so you are going to have to participate. Place your hands on your hips and rotate them backwards creating a 25-degree angle between the two straight lines of your legs and back. You are essentially bending over at the waist feeling like someone got your back belt loop and is pulling upward. Simply put, you are sticking your butt out. This is putting your hips in a position that will free them to turn more effectively.

Some of you may have been told to imitate sitting on a bar stool while at address, but I strongly disagree. This puts you into a "squatting" position which makes it difficult to create a proper hip turn. Compare the two for yourself. Remember your hips will also be in alignment and parallel to your feet. Like your feet, you do not want your hips to be open or closed. From here, unlock your knees to create a slight, but equal knee flex, and you have an outstanding lower-body set-up. Good job—you are halfway there.

Spine Angle:

Let's now consider our spine angle—the angle created between your back and legs. When rotating your hips into this position, be careful not to let your back slouch, creating a curved spine angle. Keep as straight a spine angle as possible in your set-up position. I would suggest practicing this in front of a mirror from a side angle. Once you have achieved this angle, you may want to mark your position with electrical tape on the mirror as a good reference.

I think you will feel and see that you are now in a much more athletic position. It actually reminds me of the "ready position" that is taught in tennis. The spine angle you establish at address is one that you will want to keep all the way to the top of your backswing. I will touch on this idea more once we reach the top.

Shoulder Angle:

The angle of your shoulders at address can also play a critical role in the outcome of your shot. Because your right hand is placed lower on the club than your left hand, your right shoulder should also fall below your left. This relates to the way God created us. (Again, I apologize to the left-handed golfers for having to visualize all of this backwards.)

By creating this tilted angle of your shoulders, you will sense your body is telling you to shift your upper-body position to the right of center. This is good! One of the things we will be trying to accomplish later, is to get our weight transferred to the right of center, or "behind the ball." Another way of relating to this is by putting a little more weight on the right foot. We can cheat a little bit by presetting our upper body behind the ball at address.

Are your shoulders going to be in a square position like your feet and hips? Of course, they will fall right into the parallel relationship.

Dangling Arms:

You may also notice that your arms dangle loosely in front of you if you let gravity take over. By bringing your hands together, you are ready to take your grip/soft. A lot of people want to know how far to keep their hands from their body. A good reminder is to keep the butt of the club a "hands width" from your zipper. When you start getting the club too far away from your body, you are creating too much room for potential error.

Weight Distribution:

What do you think about weight distribution in your set up? You do not want to get your weight out over your toes, but rather equally distributed in the balls of each foot. By keeping your weight on the balls of your feet, you are in a much more athletic position and better able to control your balance. The contrast is to keep too much weight on the back of your heels. With respect to the distribution of weight in each foot, it is best to try and keep it equally distributed, "fifty-fifty".

Head Position:

Let me discuss one last topic in the set-up: the head. There is one tip you will usually hear an "enthusiastic" husband tell his wife while teaching her how to play golf, which in itself can be a big mistake. The husband will tell his wife to keep her head down at all times! I know the husbands have great intentions, but this tip is absolutely incorrect. Try putting your head down with your chin resting on your chest and without moving your head, take a complete shoulder turn to the top of your backswing. What happens? Wham, you knock your shoulder right into your head, you lose your balance, and you hit a terrible shot.

So what is the correct tip we should be giving each other? Next time, tell your wife to keep her **eyes down** and her **head up**. This will allow her to keep better focused on the ball, give her room to make a complete shoulder turn, hit a nice shot, and you will probably still have dinner when you get home, if you're lucky. It is amazing what a difference keeping your eyes and not your head focused on the ball will make in your golf swing.

Even more amazing is the difference keeping your eyes focused on the Lord will make in your life. Have you had times in your life when you know you have taken your eyes off the Lord and tried to make life happen all by yourself? Are there times when you think you are big enough, smart enough, and strong enough to make it on your own? These are the times when I step back and realize I have had enough "enoughs" and turn it over to God. He is certainly **BIG ENOUGH** to handle any situation or circumstance in His own way. If we can keep our eyes focused on the Lord throughout our lives, we will be enlightened to His majesty and power.

Paul relates this so well in **Ephesians 1:17-19** when he writes, *"May the God of our Lord Jesus Christ, the Father of glory, give to you the spirit of wisdom and revelation in the knowledge of Him, the eyes of your understanding being enlightened; that you may know what is the hope of His calling, what are the riches of the glory of His inheritance in the saints, and what is the exceeding greatness of His power toward us who believe, according to the working of His mighty power."* The psalmist also related this in **Psalms 141:8** by humbling himself in saying, *"My eyes are upon You, O God the Lord; In you I take refuge."*

These are two powerful scripture references full of truth and promise. So, husbands, I hope that from now on you will be able to give your wives the tip of keeping their eyes and not their heads focused on the ball; and may all of you let this serve as a good reminder to stay focused on the Lord, taking refuge in Him.

Pictorial Review:

Here you can see Kenny Knox's set-up from the front and side views. A good way to understand what I have just described is to study a good example. So study Kenny's set-up pictorially, and then review any sections in which you were not clear. If you can copy Kenny, then you are off to a great start.

Alignment: Are You Square With God?

Someone once told me that Chip Beck, a current touring professional and one of the top-rated golfers in the world, will spend more than an hour at a time walking from behind the ball into his set-up position to master the process of establishing proper alignment. I admire his patience, and Beck may have the best set-up position in the world. However, if he is aligned improperly to his target, he will have to compensate his golf swing to direct the ball toward his target. Trust me, this results in more problems than successes, and we are smart enough to compensate our swing for alignment problems.

Beck spends over an hour looking at one golf ball. I don't know how impressive this sounds to you, but I can't withstand the temptation to hit a shot for even 10 minutes. I know I said it before, but Beck's dedication to proper alignment reiterates the necessity of standing over the ball correctly. In my opinion, Beck has a very good golf swing; one which starts with proper alignment. Let's now focus on the best way to achieve this precise alignment.

Target Line:

It is a good idea to always start your swing by facing your target from behind the ball. From here, you can see the line you want the ball to travel without having to rely on your peripheral vision. This visual line is called the **target line**. From now on, get in the habit of approaching every shot the same way until it becomes automatic.

Starting behind the ball, pick yourself a spot on the ground in front of the ball by which you can align your club. This spot can be anything from a pine needle or leaf to an old divot and will be an extension of your target line. I would not, however, pick a spot more than a foot in front of your ball. Your eyes can focus more accurately on a closer object which will minimize potential error.

Now, **keeping your eyes focused on your selected spot**, take a few steps to the left and walk to where you will take your stance holding the club in your right hand. Your path will be similar to a semicircle. Next, while keeping your stance open (your right foot square to the target line while keeping your left foot open and behind the right foot), place your club in direct alignment with your spot, and subsequently, your target. By aligning the club with your spot, you have established your target line with the club face and are ready to align your body.

Body Line:

Now that the club is ready, let's work on moving the body into place. Your body line will be parallel, or square, to your target line. It will help to visualize these parallel lines while taking your alignment. First, move your left foot forward into position, followed by the right. This rocking motion will establish balance and proper weight distribution.

Now that the foundation has been set, make sure your feet, hips, and shoulders are all square, or parallel, to your target line. You are now in a super position to take your grip and apply the set-up method you have already mastered. If you need to review, put a mark on this page and return to the section on set-up.

In support of establishing correct alignment, here is another example of how professionals give this part of their game serious attention. The next time you watch Greg Norman playing on television, pay close attention

18

to his pre-shot routine. He is very precise in emulating the routine I have just outlined. By following his example, you will establish the same kind of consistency in your game. Congratulations, you are now standing over the ball with a great set-up and alignment.

Parallel Left:

I have been discussing the parallel relationship between your target and body lines, and I know this can be confusing. When practicing your alignment and set-up routine, I would suggest using a partner. Once you get into your desired position, have your partner place one club along the line that your feet and body have established, and one in the direction that the vertical lines on your club face are pointing. Now step back from the ball, out of your stance, and take a look at the two clubs from behind. You should see that the club aligned with your club face is pointing at your target and the one relative to your body is running parallel and left of the target. Mathematically speaking, two parallel lines will never cross. If you extend these lines to the target, you will find that the body line is a few feet to the left. Does it make sense, then, that you should not line your body up to the target? I hope so, because the club face, which makes contact with and determines the path of the ball, is traveling on a different plane than the body and needs to be the object aimed at the target. Many of us find it is easy to get lined up to the right of the target which makes this adjustment feel like we are lined up two miles to the left of the target. However, it is going to take a little time for your brain to adjust to your body's change and deem this alignment acceptable. You just need to trust it and go for it; it will become comfortable with time. If there are times when you are uncomfortable standing over the ball, just back off and start over until you know it is right. Nobody ever said you have to start a shot when you do not feel good about it.

Continuing with this business of alignment, I have a question I want to pose and have you think about. How has your alignment with the Lord been lately? I know that the road to heaven is very straight and narrow, so we better be lined up straight down the middle before we start. I know that my feet tend to wander off the path, and my road is a bit more curved than I would like. How about yours? I also know my grip pressure starts to get a little tight every now and then, and I start clinging to the world looking for the wide and easy street to take. The temptations are great, and I slip and fall more times than I would like to admit. However, these are the times when I can easily look back and see that I had not kept my alignment with the Lord. One of the amazing things about this is when I find myself out of sink or misdirected, I can always link it to a lack of prayer and being out of touch with the Holy Spirit.

I long for the day when Jesus returns to walk this Earth in victory and power, yet until then He left a great teacher for us to call upon and follow: the Holy Spirit. John shares this idea with us in **John 14:25-26** by saying, *" All this I have spoken while still with you. But the Counselor, the Holy Spirit, whom the Father will send in my name, will teach you all things and remind you of everything I have said to you."*

I really like the word "remind" in this verse. It is almost as if Jesus is saying, "I know that you are going to mess up, but once you turn your eyes back on me, I will fill you with the Holy Spirit to remind you what it is like to walk parallel to the road that leads to heaven."

Steven Curtis Chapman sings, "There is no better place on earth than the road that leads to heaven." While no one ever said it was going to be an easy road to follow, with proper alignment and a great teacher to call on when we go astray, it is certainly well worth it. Like your alignment in golf, your alignment with the Lord needs to be worked on with diligence and regularity.

The squaring-up of your feet, hips, and shoulders at address can be likened to coming into a parallel relationship with the Lord, with the target being the cross of life. The path may be difficult, but great is the reward. Work on falling into the parallel slots of Christ's alignment, and then wait for the ride that will follow. It will be like no golf shot you have ever hit in your life—tap-in birdie every time.

Vision:

Have you ever been blessed with a vision from God like the bright light that converted Paul? Has the Lord ever opened the door to heaven just enough to give you a peek at what awaits you? How about a little whisper of His voice to give you the assurance you need when facing a critical situation?

I admit that my answer to all three of these questions is no. I have read stories, and heard first-hand accounts of people having direct contact with the Lord, but I cannot claim it for myself. However, I do consider myself a man of visions and rely on them to press on when times are tough and I simply want to quit on everyone and everything around me.

I have experienced some tough physical times in the past, but very few compare to the difficulties I had to face on a trip my church calls **"Challenge."** Challenge is a bicycle ministry. The trip involves around 70 people who travel about 300 miles in four days. Each day ends at a preselected church in a town not too far from the trail, where we give a concert of music, puppets, and drama to the church members or youth groups. Riding a bike 70 or 80 miles a day in the hot sun followed by a lengthy concert can sure leave some tired people, but the length of the day and work that goes into putting on a concert is not what puts fear into the minds of the dedicated cyclists.

Before each day begins there is always one question asked by the entire group; are there any big hills to encounter? When you are from the flats of Florida like myself, it is not a pleasant sight to come around a turn to find a hill that looks like a mountain going straight up for 10 miles.

If you want to experience a challenge, and some pain, find yourself a long, climbing hill and try to ride your bike up it without stopping. I guarantee that you will gain new respect for hills even when driving in your car and merely stepping on the gas a little harder to maintain your speed.

How does struggling up a hill relate to having a vision? Whenever we came upon one of these "Armageddon Hills," we adopted the habit of envisioning Jesus waiting for us at the top of the hill with his arms open wide ready to pour out his love on us. You will be amazed at how the power of a vision will allow you to overcome some of the biggest challenges in your life, even if it is just a hill. The vision helps us to keep our focus on the task and restrains the temptation to wander left and right, making the climb more difficult.

In the Old Testament, which my minister refers to as the "sticky pages" in his Bible, you can clearly grasp the necessity of a vision. **Proverbs 29:18** states, *"Where there is no vision, the people are unrestrained."* If we do not keep a vision of the Lord in the forefront of our lives, will we be unrestrained to the cloudy ways of the world? Will the struggle be too great? Will we ever get to the top of the mountain?

In his famous last speech, Martin Luther King shared that he had been to the mountain top and seen the promised land. He had a vision of the "table of brotherhood" where blacks and whites could join together in Christian fellowship. Dr. King had many visions, and I believe he was able to overcome many of his obstacles because of Heavenly visions. I challenge you to keep a Heavenly vision in mind no matter what it is you are facing or trying to accomplish.

It may seem unimportant, like climbing a hill on a bicycle, but through your vision you can make it to the other side. (You will be happy to know that the best thing about getting up the hill is that you are usually greeted by a nice, long downhill stretch, where you can rest your legs, coast, and fly like the wind.) God can also give you some coasting downhills in your life after he helps you get over those rough hills.

Here is another question. What kind of a visionary are you with respect to your golf game? I am not talking about sitting around all day dreaming about shooting 63 in the last round of the U.S. Open to set a course record and beat Jack Nicklaus by one shot. I am talking about actually having a vision for your golf shots. Have you ever envisioned your shot before hitting it? When you are standing behind the ball picking out your helpful spot for alignment, I want you to envision the golf shot you want to hit. Be very specific about every aspect. You should see the ball coming off the club at the perfect angle, rising to a selected trajectory, landing in a specific area, and coming to rest exactly where you want it.

Having a positive vision about the shot before you even strike it can only have a positive effect on its outcome. It is almost as if your brain is giving your muscles a "pre-game pep talk." Remember, this is as much a mental game as it is a physical one.

In concluding this section on pre-shot mechanics, I want to leave you with a story that exemplifies the power of visions.

Prisoner of War:

Major Nesmeth was a weekend golfer who generally shot in the 90s. He then completely quit playing for seven years. Amazingly enough, the next time back on the course he shot a sparkling 74. During the seven-year sabbatical, he took no golf lessons and his physical condition actually deteriorated. In fact, he spent those seven years in a small cage approximately 4 and one-half feet tall and slightly over 5 feet long. He was a prisoner of war in North Vietnam.

Major Nesmeth was in isolation for five and one half years of his confinement. He saw no one, talked to no one, and was unable to perform a normal routine of physical activities. For the first few months he did virtually nothing but hope and pray for his release. Then he realized he had to take some definite, positive steps if he was going to retain his sanity and stay alive.

Nesmeth selected his favorite golf course and started playing golf in his cage. In his mind, he played a full 18 holes every day. He played them to the smallest detail. He "saw" himself dressed in his golfing clothes as he stepped up to the first tee. He visualized every weather condition under which he had played. He "saw" the tee box, the grass, the trees, the birds, and all of the elements of a golf course.

He "saw" in precise detail the way he held his left hand on the club and the way he put his right hand on the club. He carefully lectured himself on keeping his left arm straight. He admonished himself to keep his eye on the ball. He reminded himself about taking the back swing slowly and easily. He instructed himself about a smooth down swing and follow-through on his shot. He then visualized the flight of the ball down the center of the fairway. He watched it fly through the air, hit the ground, and roll until it came to a stop at the exact spot he selected.

Nesmeth took the same length of time in his mind he would have taken on a golf course, taking each step to the ball he had just hit. Seven days a week for seven years he played 18 holes of perfect golf. Not once did he ever miss a shot. Not once did the ball ever stay out of the cup. Perfect. In the process of shooting mental golf, the Major was able to occupy four full hours of every day and maintain his sanity as a result. He was also able to do a great deal with his golf game. His story relates a great point. If you want to reach your goal, you must "see the reaching" in your own mind before you actually arrive at your goal. Remember, having the vision can play a big part in your game and the way you make your way through a sometimes hectic life.

The Big Picture:
The Full Swing

4

Are you ready to finally start swinging the golf club? I know we have gone through a lot of the technical points before the swing, and I commend you on your patience. Again, I assure you that mastering the grip, set-up, posture, and alignment will provide you with the best tools in making a good golf swing.

I have noticed, in teaching and playing with many different people, that there is a common way a lot of individuals try to understand the golf swing. **They simply make it too difficult.** Some golfers have been studying the game and picking up tips from every possible source for so long, that they do not know what to do with them. They figure the best thing to do is to use all of them, in the same swing, at the same time.

When teaching, I like to ask my students a lot of questions. I want to understand their perception of swing mechanics and determine the best "golf language" to which they can relate. When asking students about their full swing it is not uncommon for them to reply, "Well, I want to keep my head down, have my left arm straight here, have the emblem of my golf glove face this way here, feel a little more weight over here at this point, start to cock my wrists here, have the club pointing at the sky here, point my left knee toward 2:00 here, turn my shoulders more here, increase my body torque here, feel like I am holding a tray here, pick up my left foot here, increase the swing plane 15 degrees here, set the club with my wrists here, and remember to not let the club slip at the top. And, oh yeah, before I do all of this, I have to remember to stick out my butt and relax."

These are their swing keys for just the backswing, and they want to know if I am ready for their downswing thoughts. After wiping a look of fear off of my face, I collect my thoughts and politely tell them that they have given me more than enough information for now.

When I hear all of this, I wish God would give me a magic eraser to wipe across the minds of these poor people and clear all of these jumbled thoughts away. I cannot imagine what it is like stepping up to the first tee for a round of golf with this many ideas running through my head. It must be like trying to put together a puzzle without all the pieces. Wouldn't it be much easier to approach the mechanics of the golf swing from a more simplified angle? Remember K.I.S.S.? (Keep it simple stupid.) We are going to take one big picture and break it down into a few smaller parts, instead of taking a thousand small parts and creating one golf swing out of them all.

You know, reading back over this actually reminds me of religion. Over the years, man has managed to take God's laws, add a few thousand of his own, and jumble it into as many different religions as he can come up with that best satisfy his own needs. Everyone is running around saying my religion is better than your religion, and this rule is wrong because my rule says this. Isn't it crazy? I think God simply wanted to deliver His love to us through His son, Jesus Christ, so that we could be forgiven of our sins and receive eternal salvation.

I know this may be a simple view, but isn't this pretty much what it is all about? My minister puts it another way: "Religion is man's attempt to get close to God, while Christianity is God's attempt to get close to man."

Why are we being so selfish and making it so difficult? I saw a bumper sticker once that read, "God is too big for just one religion." Maybe this is a way of saying it is time to stop fighting over what we think is right, how we interpret one verse to the next, and keep it simple through Jesus Christ. When people ask me if I am religious, I tell them that I am not religious, but rather a Christian with a relationship with God. I think this is a pretty simple response to a big, jumbled question. What do you think?

Getting back to golf, I also think we should approach the mechanics of the swing with simple thoughts. There is clearly a lot of motion in the golf swing, and a lot of the body parts are moving at the same time. However, wouldn't it be nice if we could find a way to relate most of these movements with one major idea? I am talking about developing a mental approach to swing mechanics that will eliminate a lot of those little "tips" that confuse us more than anything.

The game of golf requires us to move the head of a golf club from the ground, into the air, back down to the ground, and make contact with a little ball. The only way to do this is to move our bodies in a way that will move the club head along a desired path. To get the club head moving along the desired path as simply as possible we will develop a **"liaison"** between our body and the golf club that will allow them to work together as one functioning unit.

The Holy Trinity:

I am sure that most of you know the Holy Trinity consists of the Father, the Son, and the Holy Spirit. The three work together in perfect unison. I hope they are working through you and your life in a powerful way. I also hope they will start working productively in your golf swing. But how can they possibly relate to my golf swing?

From a structural point of view, the golf club is designed in a particular way. The club head is connected to the neck, the neck is connected to the shaft, and the shaft is connected to the "soft." (Remember not to grip too hard.)

What is it then, that attaches the golf club to our body? We hold the soft with our hands, which is connected to our arms, which is connected to our shoulders, which is connected to the torso, and then the midsection, legs, and on down to the feet. I don't know if you picked up on the word that I have been using over and over, but everything is **connected** together. Simply put, the club is connected to our body, and when we move our body the club follows right along. Because the club head is similar to the large body parts, we can relate its path to the movement of the large muscles. Thus, the "Big Picture" idea that we are going to develop is called the **Connection Theory**. You may have heard of this before, but I have a slightly different way of approaching the theory and your golf swing. This would be from the Lord's perspective, of course. He is a pretty good teacher.

The Trinity Triangle:

As I mentioned before, we need to have a liaison, or functioning unit, to bring both the club and our body together. This is where the Holy Trinity comes into play. Looking at Kenny's set-up from the front, you can see the triangle formed between his left elbow and forearm, right elbow and forearm, and his hands. This triangle is the structure representing the liaison between your body and the club. It is essentially

27

the unit that connects your body to the golf club.

Before going into the mechanics of how the Trinity Triangle works in your golf swing, I want to first define its dimensions. A mathematical definition of a triangle is a three-sided figure connected on all sides. There can be no gaps or breaks. Mathematicians usually name the points of a triangle with letter variables such as x, y, and z. For our purposes, it is going to be better to name these points with the three dimensions of the Holy Trinity. Here is a diagram of the Trinity Triangle:

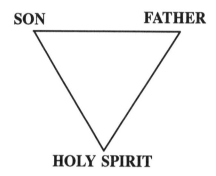

The Father, Son, and Holy Spirit are also strategically positioned for your benefit. In the seventh chapter of Acts, Stephen preaches to the council about Moses and how the Jews were resisting the Holy Spirit and the laws given to them by the prophets. The council becomes furious and is about to rush him in anger when Stephen has a vision. **Acts 7: 55-56** states, *"But he, being full of the Holy Spirit, gazed into heaven and saw the glory of God and Jesus standing at the right hand of God, and said, Look! I see the heavens opened and the Son of Man standing at the right hand of God."*

Therefore, I want you to think of your right elbow as Jesus Christ, the Son of God. With Jesus standing at the right hand of God, the Father's position is to the left of Jesus. So, I would like you to think of your left elbow as the throne of God. **I Kings 22: 19** says, *"I saw the Lord sitting on His throne, and all the hosts of heaven standing by."*

Looking at the position of the Holy Spirit, does anything jump out at you? The Holy Spirit is positioned below the Father and Son. After the death of Jesus on the cross, the Lord left behind a gift to the world. A gift we can call upon to better understand God's way. This gift is the Holy Spirit, the great teacher of spiritual things. This idea is expressed clearly in **I Corinthians 2: 12-13** with Paul's words, *" Now we have received, not the spirit of the world, but the Spirit who is from God, that we might know the things that have been freely given to us by God. These things we also speak, not in words which man's wisdom teaches but which the Holy Spirit teaches, comparing spiritual things with spiritual."* The Father and Son are busy preparing the Kingdom for eternity, yet the blessed Holy Spirit is still on the earth providing us with all of the knowledge we need. This knowledge is just a prayer away.

Feeling the Connection:

From this point on, we are going to see how the Trinity Triangle works as one unit, how the three bodies play their own special roles, and how the Trinity assists us in our golf swing and lives. I hope you are getting a strong idea of what this connection idea is all about, but now I want you to develop an idea of what the connection feels like. It is very important to transfer the thought processes of our minds to the physical reality of our golf swing. Here are some drills to start developing a feel for the connection.

Medicine Ball:

This is a good way to get a feel for the connection of the club to your body. Start by pulling your elbows in until they touch your sides. With your palms facing up, you are in a position to hold a medicine ball. (Unless you have a large ball, just use an imaginary one.) A medicine ball is very heavy and is traditionally used to develop upper-body strength. Because it is so heavy, it is very difficult to toss the ball forward with just your arm strength. However, you can make things easier if you will use some of the larger muscles of your body to support the throwing motion. You can easily toss the ball to the side if you turn your body and use your legs to support the motion. Notice that you are still keeping your elbows tucked into the side of your body.

What I really want you to feel is the way your arms and the medicine ball follow the turn of your body. Also note that the position of your arms and the ball have not changed. All you have done is turn your body while transferring weight from one foot to the other. Again, the key is that the turn of your body guided the direction of your arms and the ball by simply keeping your elbows tucked into your sides.

Now drop the ball and use the same drill with your hands together in a praying position. By turning your body and transferring some weight from one foot to the other, you are simulating the beginning motion of the golf swing. I know you may be tempted to pick up a golf club and start swinging away, but I would suggest holding off for just a minute. There are two other examples of feeling the connection I want you to look at first.

Big Rubber Bands:

Some people like to work on the connection feeling by using big rubber bands or elastic material. Have you ever seen the ads on television for the products that wrap around your arms and strap them to your body? The purpose of these products is to stabilize your arms to your body. The elastic provides a resistance that will not let your arms get away. **Therefore, the turn of your body directs the path of your arms.** I know this is beginning to sound like a broken record, but this is how simple I want you to keep it. This is actually a very good tool to have at your disposal. I noticed a few of the ladies on the LPGA Tour using it on the driving range in their warm-up sessions. You may want to buy one, or you could probably make one just as easily.

Handkerchiefs or Socks:

For this drill, you can either use two handkerchiefs or two socks. First, place a handkerchief under each of your armpits. Second, try and emulate the golf swing without letting the handkerchiefs fall to the ground. You may want to try this now. This also forces you to keep your elbows tucked in close to your side. Like the other two, this drill reinforces the connection of your arms to your body. Again, by putting your hands together like you are praying, you can simulate the first motion of the golf swing by turning your body and shifting your weight from side to side.

Connection with the Club:

Are you ready to put a golf club in your hands? Good, because the time has come. We have just finished discussing some methods to help you feel the connection. Now, I want you to transfer this feeling of connection to the golf club. The previously described tools are excellent drills to go back to. I would strongly suggest using them to warm up before practicing or playing or at home in your spare time. However, we cannot hit a golf ball very successfully with a medicine ball, so bring out your favorite weapon.

See you at the table:

Do any of you like to eat? I am not a huge eater, yet there are certain times when I am entirely focused on eating. The most obvious feeding frenzy for me is Thanksgiving dinner. When I was in college, I would dream about this glorious meal while eating in the school cafeteria. My mother always prepares a glorious meal with all the trimmings. It is quite a sight.

Dave Klan, my roommate and best friend through college, would go home with me every Thanksgiving. He had a particular craving for my mom's sweet potatoes. (He is Canadian and had never heard of or tasted sweet potatoes; especially ones topped with melted marshmallows.) The goal for Dave and me was to eat as much food over the weekend as possible, which included many late-night plates of left-overs.

The food was fabulous, but I always loved the sight of the table. The desire to dig in was great, yet I could not resist standing back for a moment to take in the sight of the table. The work my mother put into preparing the table seemed endless, yet it was well worth it.

In the last part of **John 14:2,** Jesus spoke the words, *"I go to prepare a place for you."* Can you imagine what a glorious sight this will be? I am not really sure what it will be like to be in the Lord's presence at the place he has prepared. I just know there will never be anything else to compare it to. The first part of **Psalms 23:5** shares, *"You prepare a table before me."* What kind of a feast will be prepared at the table of the Lord's house? How many courses will be served? Will there be enough for seconds and thirds? I do not have specific answers for these questions, but I am sure everyone will be content and full; especially if there are sweet potatoes covered with marshmallows like the ones Mom makes.

The feast at the Lord's table is something I look forward to, yet I want to use the table as a place for you to start your golf swing. I want you to start by standing tall, take your soft on the golf club, and hold the club straight out in front of you while keeping your elbows connected to your sides. Now imagine that the table extends well past the length of your club in front of you and to the side of you. A plane has now been created on which your club can travel. From this starting position, all I want you to do is turn your hips and shoulders. This allows the club to travel along the

31

surface of the table. It is almost like you are wiping off the top of the table with your golf club.

Please note that I want you to take the club only to a hip-high position. The club head will not be raised above the surface of the table alongside the hip. Notice that the club does not drop below the surface of the table, either. It is not possible. The table is restricting the club head from dropping below this plane. In other words, the club is being forced to stay "**in plane.**"

You can also use the analogy of a clock to grasp a better understanding of this drill. Think of your starting position as 12:00, and turn the triangle until you reach the 3:00 position. All you have to do is turn back and forth from 12:00 to 3:00.

Can you feel the connection of the club to your body via the Trinity Triangle? Has any component of the Trinity been altered? The answer is absolutely not. You have not moved the position of the Trinity from your body at all. The only thing required of you is to turn your hips and shoulders, and shift a little weight.

Can you feel how simple this is? If you have a table the right height, preferably one without a center piece, go ahead and use it. I want you to practice this motion on the "**raised**" plane several times to develop some muscle memory. You can accomplish this by turning your body back and forth with a slight weight shift. Again, the important mechanical function taking place is the club following the turn of your body **due to its connection** with the Trinity Triangle.

A New Swing Plane:

How does this drill using the table feel? I imagine it is a bit awkward. However, you will later see that the stopping point of your club at the newly created 3:00 position is crucial to the rest of your backswing. Do not worry, your muscles will soon adapt. Let's start developing the use of the Trinity Triangle from your normal set-up position. The first goal is to get the club from the starting point at address to the 3:00 position. The only difficulty is that our club is not starting at the waist-high position of the drill, but from the ground. This just changes the angle of the plane our club will be traveling on in the backswing.

If you recall, the plane we created using the clock or table did not rise or fall. It moved laterally, from side-to-side, without any slope or angle. You may remember from your geometry days that a line without any slope runs at an angle of zero degrees. As mentioned before, with the club starting on the ground, we are changing the angle on which the club will run. To get to the 3:00 position from the ground, the club has to travel "**up-and-in**" while going back. This "up-and-in" angle is essentially 45 degrees.

(*Teacher's note:* Because the big hand on a clock at the number 3 represents a quarter of an hour, I also refer to this 3:00 position as the **first quarter position.**)

Now we must apply our connection tool and let the Trinity Triangle move the club into the first quarter position. This should be a very simple motion, and I want you to make it simple in your golf swing. Just as you allowed the turning of your hips and shoulders to turn the club on top of the "**table plane**" earlier, I now want you to use the same motion with the club starting on the ground. By rotating your body and keeping the Trinity in tact, the club will follow this rotation along the desired plane.

Remember, the goal up to this point is only to reach the first quarter position utilizing the connection of the Trinity Triangle and body rotation. I know it is tempting to start taking big, full swings with the driver, but exercising patience and mastering the short steps along the way will lead to stability in your overall golf swing. Take time to practice this first move and develop the muscle memory which will lead to a solid, repetitive golf swing.

The Brick Wall:

Have you ever felt like you are just beating your head against the "brick wall of life?" No matter how hard you try, it seems like you can't get anywhere because you keep running into that same brick wall. An old roommate of mine used to come home from work and share in an energetic voice, "I could have stayed home, beat my head against the wall, and taken less of a beating than the one I received at the store today." He was a very hard-working guy, who felt like he was swimming upstream and getting nowhere. Can any of you relate to this?

Believe it or not, you can beat the head of your golf club against a brick wall, too. I call this the "**Wall of Judgment**." I mentioned before that the placement of your club at this first quarter position is crucial to the rest of the backswing.

I know I have asked this before, in reaching this first quarter position, has any member of the Trinity broken its bond from the other two members? Again, the answer is no. The triangle has retained the same geometric dimensions from address to the first quarter. The Father, Son, and Holy Spirit are still working in perfect unison together. I wish mankind could work together like this in the world, regardless of race, creed, or color. I know the Lord prefers us to exist together this way. He shares this very thought through David in **Psalms 133:1** when he writes, *"Behold, how good and how pleasant it is for brethren to dwell together in unity."*

This same message is related in **Genesis 13:8** when Abram said to Lot, *"Please let there be no strife between you and me, and between my herdsmen and your herdsmen; for we are brethren."*

I know we are human and will follow human tendencies, but it is so sad to see the way we treat each other in this world. We are so selfish and think of our own needs regardless of how we are effecting those around us. I know I have had situations in my life when I had to step back, view the situation from a different angle, and see that I was causing a lot of strife between myself and those around me. It is not easy to face up to your faults, but I know the Lord prefers us to make amends and come together as the one body of Christ he created us to be. The Holy Trinity is not breaking its unity at the first quarter position, so why not follow its example in the world we live in?

I know that He will put many brick walls in my way if I do not make the necessary efforts to develop unity with Him and the brethren of my life. There are always walls of judgment to face in life. Luckily, the "Wall of Judgment" in our golf swing will make things more pleasant. Here is how it works. When I stop the club at the first quarter position in my swing, I imagine it resting flush against a brick wall extending perpendicularly from my right foot.

The brick wall assures me that my club is **square** to the desired plane of the backswing. If you have a wall nearby that will allow you to do this, try it yourself. Notice that the club rests on a line drawn straight out from your foot and hip.

When you are practicing on the driving range, it is handy to have this line drawn for you as a good check point. You can do this by drawing a line on the grass with spray paint, or simply extend a club out from your foot. When practicing your backswing, stop the club at this point and check to make sure your club and this line match up. This will tell you immediately if you are square to the plane. Students, please take this first quarter position seriously. I believe it is one of the most important parts of the golf swing, and I relate the success of good ball striking very closely to it.

I think you will understand the squareness of the club to the plane better by looking at this position from the front and behind. In looking at these pictures of Kenny, can you see how the club would rest along the face of an imaginary brick wall? Can you also see that there has not been any distortion of his triangle to this point? This is the squareness of the club to the plane we are looking for, and it leaves us in a beautiful position to complete the rest of our backswing. This is why I refer to the wall as the "Wall of Judgment." The brick wall is a good judge of how well we are going to hit the golf ball. If we can be square with the wall, it will judge us worthy of continuing our golf swing from a good position.

This idea of comparing the brick wall to a courtroom reminds me of a statement about being a Christian: "If you were on trial for being a Christian, would there be enough evidence to convict you?" If this doesn't make you stop and think, nothing will. The truth related to this is that there will be a day when we will have to be convicted of being a Christian. When standing before the Lord, we will all be judged. **Romans 14:10c** says, *"For we shall all stand before the judgment seat of Christ."*

When the time comes, the only thing that will matter in life is whether or not the Lord convicts us of being a Christian and grants us entrance into His kingdom. It will not matter who we were, what we did, or what we had in the world. When talking about grip pressure, I related the necessity of letting go of the world and the "things" the world deems so important.

However, when standing before Christ, all these worldly things are completely irrelevant.

Are you ready to stand before Him? Is there enough evidence to convict you of being a Christian? Will the gates of Heaven be opened for you to enter? These are questions to which we all need to know the answers. I want to escape the possible judgment of the wall in my golf swing, yet I am also working on building up as much evidence of my Christianity as possible. I hope you are too.

Opening The Door:

Here is another tool to help you get to the first quarter position properly. Kenny points out that in getting to the first quarter position, you need to rotate the triangle as it is following the turn of your body. A good analogy is a door swinging open. If we were able to stand in a door frame, we could put one hand on each side of the door. This resembles our set-up when swinging the club on top of the table. To get to the first quarter, we have to rotate the door open with our arms while turning the shoulders. If you just used your left arm, it would again resemble starting at 12:00 and going to 3:00 by rotating your arm. Notice, also, that once you reach the first quarter position, the back side of your left hand is pointing straight out from the door at a 90-degree angle. It does not point down to the ground or up toward the sky. If you have an emblem on the back of your glove, this provides a good marker with which to check the rotation of your triangle.

In relation to a square position, if the emblem points down, the club face has been closed, and if it points up the club face has been open. Try it yourself and notice the differences. The main point to remember here is that the club face and shaft are being rotated into position by the turn of your body or swinging of the door.

I Will Never Leave You:

Isn't it awesome to know that Jesus will always be there for you no matter where you are or what you are doing? This is another statement of His love for all of us. This is a promise Christ makes to us in **Hebrews 13:5b** when He says, *"I will never leave you nor forsake you."* In looking at the Trinity Triangle of your golf swing, this promise is also true. If you will recall, Jesus is represented by your right elbow. If you go to the first quarter position, you will quickly see that Jesus is right there by your side.

In making my golf swing, Jesus is actually making direct contact with my side. He is right there for me and you. You can make a beautiful golf swing with your arms extended from your body, but this nice, long arc, leaves you with a lot of room for error. A longer swing is harder to control in comparison to a tighter, compact swing with Jesus right by your side. Besides, why would you want to let Jesus get away from you if you knew you could hold him close by? So when you are practicing this first move, make sure you feel Jesus by your side, and then thank him for never leaving or forsaking you.

Ouch, that hurts:

In going through this book, I will be showing you what I believe to be the right way to swing a golf club. I also want you to have a solid understanding of why things work from viewing and reading about the correct positions. However, there is also something to be said for coming to solid conclusions from understanding what not to do. You usually learn more from your failures than your successes, anyway. So continuing on in understanding this first quarter position, let's look at how a lot of golfers make common mistakes. This is when people are beating the head of their golf club against the "Wall of Judgment."

In the correct first quarter position, it has been stated that all three members of the Holy Trinity are working together in unison, without any breaks. However, what would happen if we forced the Holy Spirit to go out on His own and fight the battles without the Father and Son. Would the Spirit win the battles by himself, or perhaps cause more harm than good? Can one of the Trinity members exist on their own without the others' support? I do not have these answers, but I am glad to know that the Trinity works together as one. The problem I see in a lot of my students is that they are allowing the Holy Spirit to go out on His own when He reaches the brick wall. In physical terms, this happens when they allow their wrists or hands to break inside. With respect to the Wall of Judgment, this leads directly to a severe headache.

Judgment Time:

Here it comes! When you mess with the bull, you get the horns! The Wall of Judgment is ready to unleash its golfing fury! Let's look at this more closely from a physical perspective and see why we get into trouble. The Holy Spirit, which is represented by the hands in the Trinity Triangle, holds on to the soft/grip. If you allow your hands to break when approaching the first quarter position, the head of the golf club will smash right into the brick wall. This will not only damage your golf club, but will result in a difficult position from which to complete the rest of your swing. The main point is that **the club is no longer working in the desired plane.**

In looking back, you will see that in the desired plane, the club is resting along the face of the brick wall. If we allow the Holy Spirit to break its bond from the Trinity, you can see that the club is forced well inside the **square plane** and attempts to break through the wall.

Let's also look at what is happening to the dimensions of the triangle. Geometrically, we do not have a triangle anymore. The bending of our wrists has created two more sides for a total of five, or an odd-shaped pentagon. Spiritually, we have broken the Holy Spirit's peaceful bond with the Father and Son and allow the club to wander alone in the wilderness. Anytime we break our bond with the Father, I feel pretty safe in saying you can expect difficult times to follow. You have probably already experienced this in life, and the golf swing is no exception. So, work on keeping your hands firm at the first quarter position. This will keep your club head from smashing into the wall and keep the bond of the Trinity together.

Weight Transfer:

What is happening to our weight at the first quarter position? Without a doubt, a portion of your weight is being transferred to your right side. I have emphasized the necessity of turning your body to control the path of your club, but I want you to understand that this is a **lateral turn**. Do not confuse this with a lateral slide. I do not want you to think that swishing your hips back and forth is the way to transfer your weight. At this point in your backswing, you should feel approximately 60 percent of your weight transferred to your right side. The place where you will feel the weight and coil of your body accumulating is your right hip. This may be a new feeling to you, but it is a good one. Do you recall the idea of getting behind the ball? Well, this transfer of weight is accomplishing just that. Do not be afraid to bust out of your stationary shell and let your head and left shoulder travel over to your right a little bit. You will simply be adding to a fluid, more powerful motion.

Prophetic Golf:

"As a shepherd takes from the mouth of a lion two legs or a piece of an ear, so shall the children of Israel be taken out." **(Amos 3:12)** When you cross the Lord God enough times to really make Him mad, you better believe He can take you out if he wants to. The Lord is a loving God, but He is also a God of judgment. All through the prophetic books of **Hosea, Joel**, and **Amos**, the message to the people of Israel is very clear: Either turn from your wicked ways or face the wrath of God.

The people did not want to listen. They were having too much fun worshipping their false god, Baal. They were having too much fun committing their adulterous acts of the flesh. They were also having too much fun hoarding their gold, jewelry, and riches, while turning their backs on the poor. Worst of all, God's self-proclaimed children made no effort to follow his desire. *"For I desire mercy and not sacrifice, and the faithfulness of God more than burnt offerings."* **(Hosea 6:6)**

The people had lost faith, and their offerings were insignificant in His sight. The Lord kept warning, but they never listened. So He simply took them out. I would bet the people were not having much fun during the time of judgment. Their fond memories of Baal, sexual acts, and riches were not enough to help them survive the wrath of God. When you are taken out, that is it.

I am not going to say that hitting the Wall of Judgment is as bad as the wrath of God, but I will say it can lead to some painful golf experiences. Again, if you allow the head of your club to hit the wall by breaking your wrists inside, you are taking the club off the square plane and putting it on an inside plane. When the club gets this far inside, it leads to other bad habits, making it difficult to play good golf.

Remember, all of this results from our breaking the Holy Spirit from its bond in the Trinity Triangle. If you keep your wrists firm at the first quarter position, the Holy Spirit will not break its bond, and you won't bang your head against the wall. However, you must fight to keep the Holy Spirit/hands secure in the bond. If you are struggling and find yourself banging the wall, remember **Ephesians 4:3** as a helpful tip. *"Endeavor to keep the unity of the Spirit in the bond of peace."* With this thought in mind, I prophesy that good things are going to happen in your golfing future.

41

The Rapture

5

How has the Wall of Judgment treated you so far? Has it given you a headache, or granted smooth sailing for the future? When I think of the future, I certainly prefer smooth sailing over crashing on the rocks every time. The future used to scare me when I was a little boy. I am not referring to the future as in what you will be when you grow up, but the future as in forever. The word forever is a concept that I could not grasp. I still have a hard time with it today. Life on earth always has an end. Eventually, everything has to stop or die. Yet, I would stay awake in my bed for hours trying to imagine how long forever was. This word forever is synonymous with the mathematical term infinite. My mind would keep going and going, but there was always another number to count. There were no boundaries to how far infinite would go.

Even though I was young, I remember trying to relate this idea to heaven and hell. This is what scared me. I did not have an understanding of the Lord's salvation plan through Christ Jesus, but I did know that you either went to heaven or hell forever. I would try and imagine the pain of hell. I saw myself suffering in the fire and kept waiting for it to end. When I applied the reality of forever to this suffering, I realized life in hell would never end. I knew I wanted to be in heaven. I still did not know how to get there, but I never lost sight of the fear of hell and the necessity of getting to heaven.

I am now thankful to know of the Lord's guidelines for salvation through the death of Christ and acceptance of him as Lord and savior. I guess you could call this the Lord's "Wall of Judgment" for our lives. Just as the brick wall is a good gauge for our backswing, the Lord has determined his own measurement for our eternal salvation. This is clearly represented in **John 3:16-17**, when the Son of God shares, *"For God so loved the world that He gave His only begotten Son, that whoever believes in Him should not perish but have everlasting life. For God did not send His Son* *into the world to condemn the world, but that the world through Him might be saved."*

This guideline for salvation is the one that we cannot afford to overlook. This is the whole shootin' match. When the time comes to leave this world, your destination needs to be assured before you get there. If you are trying to get to heaven, but God puts a brick wall in your way, it is likely you will get knocked back to a place where there isn't a lot of air conditioning. However, if you maintain your **square relationship** with the Lord and do not try and run through his brick walls, he will remove the barrier letting you enter the kingdom **forever**.

I certainly do not know when the time to leave this world will be. I do not have control over life and death, and I cannot predict when the Lord is coming to get his children. I do know one thing, though. Whether it is your turn to die or the time for the Lord to snatch up his people, you need to be ready. Jesus' last words in the book of **Revelation** were, *"Surely I am coming quickly."* For those who are not ready, it will surely be too quickly.

When will the Rapture occur? Nobody knows for sure except the Father. Read these words of Christ in **Matthew 24:36-44.** *"But of that day and hour no one knows, no, not even the angels of heaven, but My Father only. But as the days of Noah were, so also will the coming of the Son of Man be. For as in the days before the flood, they were eating and drinking, marrying and giving in marriage, until the day that Noah entered the ark, and did not know until the flood came and took them all away, so also will the coming of the Son of Man be. Then two men will be in the field: one will be taken and the other left. Two women will be grinding at the mill: one will be taken and the other left. Watch therefore, for you do not know what hour your Lord is coming. But know this, that if the master of the house had known what hour the thief would come, he would have watched and not allowed his house to be broken into. Therefore you also be ready, for the Son of Man is coming at an hour when you do not expect him."* Oh yes, we need to be ready.

Air Time:

If the Rapture does occur during my lifetime, I am looking forward to fulfilling a childhood dream: being able to fly. The origin of the word rapture comes from the Greek word "harpazo," which means to snatch away or to be caught up. Paul enlightens us to what will happen to the saved still on earth during the Rapture in **I Thessalonians 4:17**. *"Then we who are alive and remain shall be caught up together with them in the clouds to meet the Lord in the air. And thus we shall always be with the Lord."*

This ascent is actually the next idea I want to express in your backswing. We have established a solid position at the wall of the first quarter, and it is now time to continue the ride to the top along the vertical plane. For obvious reasons, this part of your backswing will be referred to as the Rapture.

The Meeting Place:

What method did we utilize to rest the club squarely against the wall in the first quarter position? Did we simply pick up our hands and put them there? The answer is obviously, no. By utilizing our connection of the Trinity Triangle, we are able to move the club squarely to the plane by **the turning, or rotation, of our body**. If this method has been effective up to this point, wouldn't we want to continue using it to the top of our backswing? Absolutely! You will find that regulating a fluid and complete turn throughout the entire swing is a major component to your golfing success. I must emphasize the importance of continuing the turn of your hips and shoulders from the first quarter position throughout the Rapture section of your backswing. However, there are a few mechanical ideas and changes to the Trinity Triangle I want to share with you along the way.

Holy Spirit Hinge:

Chuck, what in the world are you suggesting here? Has the Holy Spirit gone into the carpentry business with Jesus by attaching itself to the frame of a door? No, this is not what I am suggesting at all. Rather, I am suggesting it is time for your hands to begin hinging toward the top of the swing. As I mentioned before, it is time to start working the club up the vertical plane. This also requires the members of the Trinity to be raptured and working more vertically. First, let's look at what is happening to the Holy Spirit, or hands. As the club is passing through the first quarter position, the hands are going to begin a cocking or hinging motion which you will feel in your wrist.

This hinging motion actually encompasses two movements simultaneously. First, the hands will be hinging upward. If you had a

45

hammer in your right hand and were going to strike a nail, you would have to hinge the hammer vertically with your hand before driving the nail into the wood. This is similar to what is happening with the golf club.

The second half of this movement is a slight rolling of the hands to the right. I am not talking about laying the club off as flat as a board, but rather a roll that follows the rotation of your arms. This rotation was expressed earlier in the drill of opening the door. To better explain this motion, let me describe a position that will serve as an excellent checkpoint in your backswing. I call this position the **meeting place**.

Before sharing this position with you, I must first give credit to the man who taught it to me, Bill Skelley. Bill is an excellent teaching professional and runs one of the finest golf schools in the country. I have been fortunate enough to teach with him on several occasions. The meeting place position is halfway between the brick wall and top of your swing. In order for your club to remain square to the plane going to the top, the club must be angled at a 45-degree angle. Bill likes to describe it as the club resting on a **slant**. This slanting plane results from addressing the ball with the club slanted. If we were able to stand directly over the ball and swing the club like a pendulum, our plane would be very steep and almost completely vertical. Perhaps a better phrase to use for this "Rapture" section of the backswing is the **slanted plane**.

Bill also has an excellent tip from which to check the angle of your club at this position. Imagine an extended line coming out the butt end of your golf club. (You can create this extended line by simply gripping the club in the middle of the shaft.) If you have positioned your club properly on the slant, the extended line will come to rest on the ground at your original target line. Remember, the target line runs from behind the ball directly to the target.

This extension of your club will immediately tell you if you are working on the slanted plane. If the club is too steep, the extension of the club will hit the ground away from your target line closer to your feet. Conversely, if the club is too flat, the line will contact the ground several feet away from your body and the target line. In practicing this drill, you may find it necessary to call upon a friend to extend the line while you pose in the position. You may also want to have another club on the ground representing your target line. If your slanted line is not pointing at the target line, make the adjustments until they line up.

Bill demonstrates the extended line of the club during his lectures by using a poll with a flashlight on the end of it. When the lights are turned out you can see how the ray of light points at the target line when the club is on the proper slant. If the club is not slanted correctly, the ray of light will tell you if you are too flat or too steep, and you can easily make the necessary adjustments. If you ever run into Bill, ask him to show you his flashlight tip and tell him I said hello.

Remember, turning the club on the slanted plane encompasses two moves. The first is the turning of your shoulders. Not breaking down the turn of your shoulders is a big key. The second is the hinging of the wrist with a slight roll attached to it. Something to note is the short distance the club travels to get from the first quarter position to the meeting place. The hands, or Holy Spirit, are only traveling from a "hip high" to "chest high" location. This is only a matter of eight to 10 inches. The wrists are beginning to hinge, but it is a very simple motion.

Checking the Holy Trinity, you may have noticed that the Trinity Triangle has undergone some slight changes at the meeting place position. We have already discussed the changes in the Holy Spirit, and the changes in the Father and Son are a little more subtle. Upon reaching the meeting place position, you will find a slight gap between your elbows and your side. Do not worry, this is fine. At the brick wall, I actually have contact of my right elbow, or Son, with my side. However, since we are working the club on a slanted plane, the Father and Son will work up the slant as well. You will find that this occurs naturally and does not require much effort. It would be very difficult to keep the Father and Son physically attached to your side throughout the entire backswing. I guess you could do it, but you may find it very painful.

Try this for yourself. If you keep your elbows tucked in at your side while turning past the first quarter position, the club will travel flat to the plane, and it probably hurts your back. So, don't worry about the natural gap that the Father and Son have extended from your side. They are still working close to you.

Even though I do not keep the Lord Jesus in physical contact with my side throughout the entire backswing, an important swing key of mine is to keep Him very close and connected. I do not want one of those flying right elbows which lets Jesus get far away from me. By keeping Him tucked in close to me, He helps to keep my club square to the plane. If I push Jesus away from me, I have created a lot of room for error in my life and golf swing. So, when checking your position at the meeting place, expect the Father and Son to have a slight gap from your side, but know that they are still connected and working hard to keep you in proper alignment.

I'm sure you are wondering about the meaning behind this meeting

I apologize for not yet explaining it, but I had to save the best for last. Recall with me **I Thessalonians 4:17.** *"Then we who are alive and remain shall be caught up together with them in the clouds to meet the Lord in the air. And thus we shall always be with the Lord."* This verse states that the saved will first be caught up to meet the Lord in the air. Before going home to the kingdom, we will have a little pit stop to make first. This is the half-way point between our time on earth and heaven. This pit stop is the meeting place I am referring to in your golf swing. You have survived God's judgment at the brick wall, and are now half way to the top. Congratulations, you are almost home.

Weight Transfer:

What is happening with our transfer of weight? Remember that we had shifted approximately 60 percent our weight to the right side at the first quarter position. Are we going to continue this lateral, turning motion? Of course. At the meeting place position, you will feel about 75 percent of your weight on your right hip and leg. It may feel a little uncomfortable right now, but all of the force being stored up from this **lateral turn** will be very useful for the downswing. Do not be afraid to let your left shoulder travel a bit to the right behind the golf ball. This follows right in line with your lateral turn. You just have to trust the movement if you have never done it before. Besides, you are not going to believe how much farther you will hit it. Sorry, just a little insight to the future.

Learn From Your Mistakes:

At the first quarter position, I showed you a very common mistake: breaking your hands inside and banging your club against the wall. This places the club way inside the plane which leads to many more problems. Well, here is one of them. If the club is traveling to the meeting place from an inside position at the first quarter, it usually follows a different path: a very **steep** one. The hands do not have much of a choice but to climb the ladder and head up. If you apply Bill's extended line test to this plane, you will see how steep it is. You have probably seen golfers who can play pretty good golf from this position, but a lot of good adjustments have to be made to combat these bad habits before playing good golf. So, let's remember to stay square at the Wall of Judgment and allow the club to work on the slanted plane at the meeting place.

Going Home:

Here it is. This is the moment we have been waiting for. The struggles of the world have been left behind, and the pain and suffering have been worth it. This is why Paul said, " *to die is to gain"* in **Philippians 1:21**. The gates to the Kingdom of Heaven are being opened and we have a ticket with "admission" stamped on it. By following His word and enduring the struggle, we are able to share the home that Christ promises to us. (See **John 14:2**.)

Christ solidifies his promise even further by claiming, *"If anyone loves Me, he will keep My word; and My Father will love him, and We will come to him and make Our home with him"*. (**John 14:23**) What is it going to be like to be a part of the Body of Christ as we are flying through the air making our way to the kingdom? Will a silver lining break open in the clouds to show us the way home, or will Christ use his sword to slash out the silver lining, piercing the darkness of hell and leading to the gate of heaven? I don't know. All I know is that we need to be a part of the vehicle when the whistle blows. Once you see the silver lining, the path should be clear. Going home will be the easy part.

Believe it or not, your position at the meeting place provides the silver lining you need. The path is clear and the doors to heaven are being opened. All you have to do is follow the silver lining and rush into the arms waiting for you. Let me expound upon this in mechanical terms.

At the meeting place, your club is resting upon a slanted plane at a 45-degree angle, and the extended line of the club is pointing at the target line. I just stated that all you have to do from here is follow the path of the silver lining and you will make it home to the kingdom. What is the silver lining? It is simply the **shaft of the club** laying on the slant. From a color perspective, this works well because most club shafts have a silver color. However, I am more concerned with the path it represents. Look at the following diagram .

50

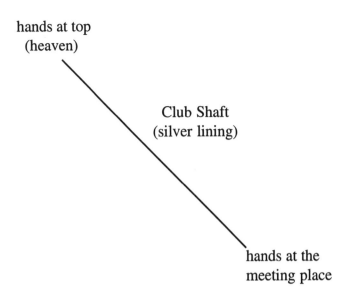

hands at top
(heaven)

Club Shaft
(silver lining)

hands at the
meeting place

You can see that the diagram represents two positions of the hands: at the meeting place and at the top of the backswing. You may have also figured out that we need to get our hands from the meeting place to heaven. How do we get there? We follow the silver lining by continuing the turn of our hips and shoulders. By continuing to turn, **the hands follow the path created by the slant of the club into the proper position at the top of the swing.** This works for the same reason we have discussed from the beginning of the swing. The connection you have established in the Trinity Triangle follows the turn of your body.

Here is another drill to help you see how this works. (You will need a partner.) Take your backswing to the meeting place position and stop. Check the position of the club making sure it is on the proper slant. Next, have a friend hold the club on the slant you have just established, so you can let go of the club entirely. With the club remaining on the slanted plane, rest your hands at the approximate location where you would take your grip/soft, and let your hands follow the path of the club shaft by completing your turn. By following the "silver lining," your hands are being led along the path to the top of the backswing, which is called **heaven.** All you are doing is following the desired plane without a club in your hands. This is accomplished by continuing to turn and letting the connection do the rest.

Trinity check:

It is again time to check the Holy Trinity and see how they are working in our golf swing. Quite honestly, there has not been much change from the meeting place position. In reaching the top, or heaven, the Holy Spirit remains in its cocked position. Your wrist may cock a little bit more, but the weight of the club will aid this motion if necessary. Are the Father and Son still with you? Absolutely! In looking at the position of the right elbow, you can see and feel how nicely it remains tucked in by your side. One of the greatest things about the Trinity Triangle is the way the Lord Jesus Christ never leaves your side throughout the backswing. You will find that He stays with us throughout most of the downswing as well. Do not forget to thank the Trinity for guiding you safely into the kingdom. They have had a lot to do with it. Thanks, Dad.

Weight Transfer:

We would not want to forget about this important factor, but do we have any more weight to transfer? How about 15 percent more for a total of 90 percent. At the top of your backswing, you have loaded up a tremendous amount of weight on the right side. How will you know if it is enough? I have another drill for you. If you have transferred enough weight to your right side at the top of the swing, you should be able to pick up your left foot. What will happen if you pick up your left foot without transferring enough weight? You will fall over. This drill is to practice getting to the top of your swing, picking up your left foot, and then continuing with the downswing. This will require some rhythm, but it will help develop the feeling of getting your weight over to your right side.

What about head movement? A lot of people think you should keep your head perfectly still throughout the entire swing without allowing any lateral movement. My question to these people is, "How are you going to transfer weight behind the ball if your head is stationary?"

Your body follows the movement of the head, thus it is necessary to allow the head to move behind the ball if you expect your body to also. The key in transferring your weight is that it coincides with the lateral turn of your body. I am not looking for a sliding motion without any turn, nor am I going to say there is an exact distance your head needs to move. It may be three inches for one person, and six inches for another.

I remember watching the Masters several years ago, and they showed an overhead view of Ben Crenshaw's swing from address to the top of the backswing. They drew lines on the screen marking the before and after head positions, and revealed that Crenshaw's head moved a good six inches. Again, the key is that he never stopped turning his body. I want you to establish what is comfortable for you, as long as the weight is being transferred and the turn completed.

Wind it up:

Are any of you having trouble getting turned all the way to the top of the swing? I think you would agree that a full turn helps with distance, keeps the club on plane, and produces a beautiful golf swing. However, I know that some of you have a hard time getting turned all the way to the top. Some people use lack of flexibility, age, or anything else they can come up with as an excuse for not turning as far as they should. I know that some cases are 100 percent legitimate, but I would bet most of us can turn farther if we push it just a little bit.

When looking at the degree of turn desired, I am not asking for one as large as John Daly, where you can almost see behind you. Rather, I want everyone to get their shoulders and hips turned enough to make a full backswing. What I am suggesting is stretching out and using some muscles that have not seen action for a while. I know this does not happen over night, so I have an idea that will be quite useful.

I try to stay in pretty good shape, and I often find myself either in the gym or sweating some pounds off in aerobics class. One of the tools used in the aerobics class is an elastic tube, which provides resistance to the stretching of the muscle.

With this in mind, here is your golf/aerobics workout tip. Take the ends of the tubing in each hand and step on the middle of the tube with your left foot. Next, take your golf grip while holding onto the ends of the tube. The tube will hang limp at the set-up position, but as you take your backswing, you will find that the tube draws tight and begins to resist your turn. In order to extend the tube all the way to the top, you will have to provide more strength in the turn. The more you practice this exercise, the more strength you will build up in the "turning muscles," and you will soon have a full backswing.

If you want to provide more resistance to the tube, simply grip lower on the tube. So, if you are having difficulty making that full turn to the top, try the golf/aerobics tip and stretch out those muscles. Who knows, this idea of golf/aerobics may become the latest fitness craze.

Spine Angle:

Here is a term we have not talked about in a long time. If you recall from the section on set-up, we established a spine angle between our back and legs. I also mentioned that you would want to keep this same spine angle to the top of your swing. Here is why. If you begin straightening your body on your way to the top, you are altering the plane on which you are swinging.

This would not be a big problem if the ball would rise up off the ground at the same angle that you are lifting your body. Most people increase their spine angle by lifting their head in the backswing, which in turn lifts the body. I have also found that this causes people to lose their visual focus on the ball. When they get to the top of their backswing, they have lost complete sight of the ball. This forces them to refocus on the ball coming back down in order to make contact. Also, if you pick your body up on the way back, you are going to have to drop it back down on the way through. If you have ever hit a fat shot, this might be part of the problem.

If you are lifting out of your original spine angle, try to feel like you are staying low to the ball all the way to the top of your backswing. This will cause your head to stay in position going back, solidify your spine angle, and allow you to work into the ball from the proper plane. This will feel like an exaggerated move at first, but it will become comfortable with a few swings.

When utilizing the mirror as a tool to check posture, I suggested placing some tape on the mirror to establish your spine angle. The tape also provides a good mark to check your spine angle at the top. If your spine angle is pretty close to matching the tape on the mirror, you are in good shape. If the angle has become too severe and you are not matching the tape on the mirror at all, then you will know to work on maintaining your spine angle all the way to the top. Remember to let your club work up the vertically slanted plane, and not your body.

Welcome to Heaven:

Congratulations, you have finally made it. It has been a long journey, the struggle was great, and the battle tough. However, the reward is worth it. In reaching the top of the backswing, you have reached the upper echelon: heaven. Through the gift of salvation at Calvary, the Lord Jesus Christ has brought you home to live with him forever. In reaching the top, I want to go over a few check points to make sure everything is in order. Seeing is believing, so I want you to see a front and side angle of Kenny's swing at the top. Looking at the view from the front, here is a list of things I want you to notice:

1. a complete turn of the hips and shoulders
2. excellent transfer of weight behind the ball
3. head has moved laterally behind the ball
4. left shoulder has traveled to the right behind the ball
5. club has not dropped past parallel

From behind:
1. again, notice the full turn of hips and shoulders
2. spine angle has remained the same having not lifted up
3. compactness of his triangle and connection
4. Lord Jesus, or right elbow, is in tight by his side
5. hinging of the Holy Spirit has set club to parallel at top
6. position of club is pointing "parallel left" of target

Watching Kenny hit balls in person, or looking at pictures of his swing, leaves no doubt that he has a beautiful golf swing. It is also a swing that has been developed with countless hours of practice. However, you need to believe that you are well on your way to making beautiful golf swings. I know you can do it. Besides, reaching heaven can be nothing else but beautiful. The great thing about your golf swing is that it allows you to reach heaven twice in one swing. So keep that in mind as we get started on the other half of the golf swing. There is a lot of exciting things to look forward to.

More mistakes:

I hate to end the first half of the swing on a sour note, but we have some unfinished business to take care of. I need to complete the picture of what happens when you bang the head of your golf club against the Wall of Judgment. At the meeting place, we saw that the club was getting very steep and working away from the slanted plane. Unfortunately, it doesn't get any better from here. Upon reaching the top, the club points to the far right of your target and has crossed the boundaries of "parallel left." The Holy Trinity is still working out of plane, and the Lord Jesus is actually beginning to fly out on his own a little bit. Satan is getting more and more control of your swing, and he is laughing at the possibilities of you hitting a good shot.

Since I am discussing a sour note, let me throw another one at you. Do you know what happens if you do not transfer your weight to the right side, behind the ball? You become a dipper, and I am not talking about chewing tobacco. You have kept too much weight on your left foot, your head has not moved, and your left shoulder has dipped toward the ground. You may be more familiar with the phrase reverse pivot or something else, but you are clearly a dipper.

If you have both problems of hitting the brick wall and being a dipper, Satan is licking his chops. However, we are going to take care of this evil character later on. Also, you now have the understanding to make the necessary corrections in your backswing and turn around to bust Satan in the chops. We all have some problems to overcome, but the helping hand of the Lord will make it that much easier. It is going to take some time and practice, but I know you can do it. Again, congratulations on making it to heaven. The fairways sure are wide and green, aren't they?

Tribulation : The Downswing

Wait a minute. Are you trying to tell me that after enduring all of the hard work, suffering trials, and difficulties of the world, you want me to leave heaven and go back to all that I left behind? You want me to walk back through the pearly gates, put my membership on hold, and take the elevator to the ground level? You want me to give back my crown, hang up my robe in the closet, and tell Moses we can finish the back nine when I return? (Chuck, I was seven under and lining up a makeable eagle putt on the eleventh). Well, kinda-sort-of, in a round-about-way, yes. But you have to remember I already told you that you get to go back after taking care of one small detail: **Satan**.

After the Rapture and our emergence in heaven, Satan is working harder than ever. He knows that he doesn't have much time before the King comes back to claim what is rightfully his, so he is working double time. From a spiritual point of view, I am talking about the Tribulation. In golfing terms, I am describing the first section of your downswing. I bet you never thought you would have Revelation revealed to you through golf instruction. Well, hold on to your hat, because it is just going to get better. There is some unfinished business to take care of back on earth, and my main man, Jesus Christ, has got the right plan of attack. So, with the hour of the Tribulation upon us, prepare yourself for some spiritual warfare and the unleashing of tremendous power. The King is coming.

Beginning the Downswing:

Let me begin with a quick summary of where we left off. We have arrived at the top of our backswing with the club in plane, an excellent transfer of weight, and a full turn of the hips and shoulders. We have a veritable plethora of potential energy stored within the framework of our body and the end of the golf club. Now what do we do with it? Don't you just hit the ball and go on to the next shot? Not quite. I wish it were that easy, but there are a few things to consider.

Unfortunately, a lot can go wrong from the top of the backswing to impact, which results in many misdirected shots. However, we can avoid all of this by keeping a few solid points in mind.

Pull it Down:

When referring to the path of the club in the backswing, I introduced the idea of letting it work on an **"up and in"** plane. Because of the angle of the club at address, it travels up and in on its way to the top. Does it make sense then, that we would want our club to work **"down and out"** on its way to impact? I hope so, because this is one of the most important mechanical properties I can share with you in the downswing. With this in mind, I want to focus on the "down portion" of this idea first.

The Holy Spirit and Son are doing some strong work in the first movement of the downswing. What I want you to feel when initiating your downswing is a **pulling of the hands** down toward the ball. Remember, this portion of the downswing is the onset of the Tribulation, the antichrist is rising in power, and great destruction will take place. **Revelation 6:1-2** relates the action of the antichrist in the opening of the first seal. *"Now I saw when the Lamb opened one of the seals; and I heard one of the four living creatures saying with a voice like thunder, "Come and see." And I looked, and behold, a white horse. And he who sat on it had a bow; and a crown was given to him, and he went out conquering and to conquer."*

Yes, the Lord has granted permission to the antichrist momentarily to gain power and to conquer. Do not fear, it is all in the Lord's hands. The Lord has stored up his power and will unleash it in his perfect timing. This is exactly what we are doing in the golf swing.

Essentially, you are keeping all of the force built up in the golf club stored for later use. By pulling down with the hands, you are forcing the hands to lead the club head. Let the Holy Spirit lead while the club head lags behind. Again, this aids in generating more force to be unleashed through impact and upon Satan at the Lord's perfect time.

Unwinding the Turn:

It is now time to figure out how to utilize the full turn of the hips and shoulders generated to the top of the backswing. Let me use an illustration to help find the answer. Do you remember the model airplanes you used to build as a kid that would fly after you wound up the rubber-band-powered propeller? What would you do after you wound up the propeller as tight as it would go? Simple, you just let it go and watched the plane take flight. This is similar to the potential energy we have stored up in the turn of our body. All we have to do is unwind the turn and let it go. However, I need to remind you that I am still discussing the first move of the downswing, and the unwinding of the turn coincides with the pulling of the hands. They are both happening at the same time. With this in mind, let's see how the hips and shoulders unwind in this first move.

First, the hips and shoulders begin the downswing by turning back into the ball. We have successfully used the turning of our body to guide the path of the club to the top via the Trinity Triangle, and we are most certainly going to use it on the way back down. I know some of you are saying, "But if I try to turn my shoulders from the top of the backswing, I am going to come right over the top and hook it out of bounds." This is actually a good concern to have. However, remember that I stressed the importance of the turning motion coinciding with the leading of the Holy Spirit. If your hands are leading the club head down the plane, the turning of your hips and shoulders will not throw the club over the top and out of plane. I think you will find that the unleashing of the turn will be very natural. It is the pulling of the hands that will require more effort to master.

Not So Fast Upper Body:

I already introduced the idea of a lead/lag relationship between the hands and club head in the pulling motion of the Holy Spirit. This relationship can also be found between the hips and shoulders in the **transfer of weight** throughout the downswing. I also refer to this as a relationship between the upper and lower bodies. In the backswing, both the upper and lower body weights are transferred to the right side at pretty much the same time. There really isn't a noticeable separation. However, things change slightly on the way down. This is where the lead/lag relationship comes into play. In this case, the lower body is leading while the upper body is lagging behind. In looking at the lower body, you will find that its first move is to shift about 50 percent of its weight back to the left side. Most of this weight is felt in the left foot.

Just as I did on the backswing, let me emphasize that this weight transfer is not a lateral slide. Rather, it is a lateral turn. You are putting weight on the left side, but it is not accomplished by throwing your left hip into the ball like one of Elvis' gyrations. Remember, Elvis is not the King of Kings, so we do not need to emulate him in our golf swing. Do you remember my instruction on keeping your left foot turned slightly open at address? I wanted you to do this so you could clear your hips out on the way through. You clear your hips out by turning them through the downswing, not by sliding.

The lagging member in this relationship is the upper body. The upper body clearly follows the lower in the weight transfer on the downswing. It will probably feel like the upper body does not move laterally at all if you are used to making an aggressive drive into the ball with your upper body. Your upper body needs to be the calm, cool, and collected member of the two. It cannot be in a hurry to wipe out Satan during the Tribulation hour. Remember, the Lord is in control and will take care of him at the right time. Our human instinct wants everything right now, but we have to exercise patience to allow the Lord's will to be perfect. Do not worry, the upper body will have its time to catch up and shine in glory.

Trinity Update:

Once again, we need to check on the Holy Trinity and see what they are doing in our golf swing. During the Rapture, we noticed a slight separation of the Trinity from our side as they worked up the slanted plane. Well, it is time to reel them back in close to our side.

We have already looked at the action of the Holy Spirit. He is pulling back down the slanted plane, adding to the amount of force being generated in the club head. Thankfully, the Father and Son are also working down the slanted plane. This relocates them into a position by our side. If you are having trouble picturing what I mean by the members of the Trinity working back down the slanted plane, this is a good time for a pictorial comparison. I want you to compare the positions of Kenny's triangle at the top of his backswing and the first move of his downswing. Can you see how the right elbow, or Son, has dropped down right by his side? If you could transpose one on top of the other, you would be able to draw a line almost straight down in connecting the two points of his elbow. You will be glad to have them tucked back in close to your side working with you.

In looking back, I realize that I have not given this position a name. Because we are in the midst of the Tribulation battling the rise of the antichrist, I am going to call this position your "**Battle Station.**" Our forces are strong and ready to make the final attack. When the trumpet sounds and Christ is ready to reclaim the world, the saved in Christ had better man their battle stations and be ready for a glorious victory. Get ready people, the time is coming soon when we get to unleash this force stored in the club upon the head of Satan himself.

Now that we have a name for this first position of the downswing, let's look at it a little closer from a mechanical view. I want you to start your downswing, and stop at your battle station. Make sure the hands are pulling while the hips and shoulders are turning, and the upper body lags behind the lower. Does this position feel familiar to you? What other part of your golf swing can you correlate this to? How about the meeting place position? You have already mastered this position going back. These two positions are not identical; the path going down works a little more from the inside, but can you feel and see the similarities? The Trinity is in relatively the same place, and the club is working down a similar slant close to the one it worked up.

If we want the club head to return to the ball in pretty much the same place from which it started, it should follow approximately the same path. This is like finding your way home when you are lost. You find a familiar path and follow it. (This resembles the straight and narrow path Jesus gives us to follow when we are lost and want to get home.) When posing at your battle station, check the similarities to the meeting place and know that you are on the right path to get back home to heaven.

Here Fishy, Fishy, Fishy:

Are there any fishermen out there? If you are like me, you have thrown a few lines around the lakes of a golf course before. There is nothing quite as exciting as having a large-mouth bass explode onto your bait and reel off 50 feet of your line.

I remember once when I was about 10, my dad took me fishing at Lake Okeechobee in south Florida. It was getting late in the afternoon on the first day, and there had not been much action. I was getting pretty bored and tired. Our guide, Herman, had me rigged with a wild shiner and a plastic bobber. This did not mean much to me because I didn't know what a shiner was, and I was falling asleep on the bow.

Needless to say, I was not paying much attention to fishing, and I was unaware that my shiner had become very excited and was frantically dragging the bobber behind it. Out of nowhere, a cannonball drops out of the sky in the form of a large-mouth bass. It swallows my shiner, takes off toward the weeds, and pulls my fishing rod, with me attached to it, over the side of the boat. Luckily, Herman caught me by the back of my pants and saved me from swimming with this monster. I was now awake. I began reeling with all my might. The hook was firmly set, and I was closing in on him. He made it to the weeds, but Herman had pulled up the anchor and we were tracking him into the middle of the cat tails. Surely this was a new world record. It had to be. I was going to be famous. My picture would be on the front page of all the magazines.

All I had to do was reel this monster in, and my life would never be the same. And then it happened. The worst thing that a young angler could ever dream about—the line broke and the big one got away. Devastation quickly set in. I was 10 feet from all the glory, and the monster bass snapped the line like a piece of chalk. Herman tried to console me by saying that from the size of the explosion, he was sure it weighed at least 15 pounds, probably more. Despite his genuine effort, it did not help. Just like that, the life-changing moment was taken away from me.

But, it doesn't end there. It is like the commercial of the little kid all by himself on the play-ground, taking the last shot for the championship of the entire world. The shot goes up, it hits the rim, bounces around, and misses. After a short pause and thinking over the situation, he announces to the world, "But he was fouled." You can't keep a good man down for long. Just like this little kid, the game wasn't over, and I had another chance at victory.

Aren't you glad God gave us another chance to win the victory over life and death? The world is messed up, but God says here, take my son, accept him as Lord and Savior, and you can have the victory of eternal life. We are all born sinners and are unworthy of admission to heaven, but God loves us enough to give us a second chance. He gives us another chance to make a free throw. He gives us another chance to make the three footer to win the Masters. He gives us another chance to live with Him forever through the blood of the Lamb. Thanks for being and giving me a second chance, Dad. I really appreciate it.

It is true that in my fishing story the big one got away. However, that was not the end of the day, and there was more fishing to be done. Now that I was awake, I was ready for the next one. Herman tied another hook on the line, baited another shiner and bob, and I was back in the fishing saddle. My first cast could have landed on a dime. It didn't take long. The shiner began squirming around in the water, and bam, another bass had shown up for dinner. This time the hook was set quickly, and the bass had no chance of fleeing into the weeds. This one was reeled in quickly, and it was certainly a keeper. Within 30 minutes, I had reeled in five bass totaling close to 40 pounds. My dad and Herman were so excited they forgot to do some fishing themselves. It did not matter, they were having enough fun watching me reel them in.

Back at the dock, all the people gathered around to see the large string of fish. Everyone wanted to know where we had found them, but Herman smiled as he said, "Oh, just a mile or so toward the west." Every good fisherman knows you cannot reveal your best spots. Despite knowing that the monster of all monsters had gotten away, it still turned out to be a grand afternoon for a 10-year-old kid.

I didn't miss taking advantage of my second chance while fishing or in life. I guess I got lucky on both accounts. The Lord waited on me to come around until I was 23 years old. I was out doing my own thing, having fun with the boys, and trying to please the world. My life was pretty good compared to most others, but the peace was missing. Again, I am thankful Dad waited on me long enough to grasp the second chance he had for my life. I hope you take advantage of the one God has for your life, too.

You may not believe it, but this fishing story is true. OK, maybe I wasn't actually being pulled overboard, but Herman did have a hold of my pants just in case. Besides, a fishing story would not be a fishing story without a little exaggeration.

I sometimes wonder what kind of exaggerated fishing stories some of the disciples told in their day. It turns out that seven of the 12 disciples were fishermen. If I had to lay money on one of the 12, I would probably claim Peter as the most questionable story teller. He certainly seems, to me, to have been the most talkative of the bunch. After feeding the 5,000, Jesus instructed the disciples to get in the boat and meet him at the other side. When the storm arose and they were in great fear, Jesus walked out on the water to them and said, *"Be of good cheer! It is I; do not be afraid."* (**Matt. 14:27**) Peter was the first to answer Him and said, *"Lord, if it is You, command me to come to You on the water."* (**Matt. 14:28**) The disciples were in a boat, in the middle of a storm, and concerned for their safety. When Jesus approaches them on the water, they are in fear crying out, *"It is a ghost."* (**Matt. 14:26**) Yet Peter immediately speaks up, and in a bold voice questions if he is really the Lord because he wants to walk on the water with him. This is a man who is not afraid to speak his mind. Without hesitation, he jumps out of the boat and walks on the water toward Jesus. I feel pretty confident that Peter would be the one to talk about the one that got away in somewhat exaggerated terms.

Some of you may not like to fish and have never had a need to tell a far-fetched story. However, some of you go fishing on the golf course with every round you play. Remember in the backswing when I taught you what not to do by learning from your mistakes? Well, it continues with the downswing. The big problems I shared with you in the backswing were banging your club head against the wall, getting the club way inside the plane, and having it point well right of your target at the top of the swing. You have gotten yourself in big trouble, and you have to find some way out.

If you pull your hands down from the top as previously prescribed, you will be fighting from so far inside it will take the strength of John Daly to get the club head through at impact. (By the way, this is actually the way John Daly swings the club. He is way inside the square plane from the beginning, but he has enough strength in his turn and hands to get the

club head through at impact. I do not recommend trying it yourself.)
Because most people do not have this kind of strength and flexibility, they
have to resort to another method of getting the club through: they go fishing.
The term most teaching professionals are familiar with is "**casting**."

If you were actually out fishing, you would cast your rod by breaking
your wrist through as your arm extended forward. The tip of the rod whips
ahead of the hands, throwing your line and lure into the water. This is
great technique for fishing, but not so good for golf. Jesus did say, *"Follow
Me, and I will make you fishers of men"* in **Matt. 4:19**, but notice that he
did not tie in the idea of playing golf with fishing. Some people may
interpret this verse differently from others, but I doubt the subject of the
golf swing has ever been brought up when looking at this verse.

As a refresher, the reason I want you to pull your hands in a downward
motion from the top is to get the club working back into the ball on plane.
This motion also increases the amount of force the club head will exert
into the ball at impact. By contrast, if you are casting the club from the
top, you achieve the opposite effect. The simplest way to describe the
casting motion is that the wrists start to break in the first move of the
downswing. The result is the club being forced to work outside the plane
and all of the force that had been stored up is thrown away.

This motion is also referred to as "club head throwaway." Just as the
tip of the rod passes your hands very early while casting a fishing rod, this
casting of the golf club allows the club head to pass your hands much too
early in the golf swing.

I want you to compare these two motions for yourself. First, start the
downswing by pulling the Holy Spirit down the plane, and feel the Father
and Son working close to your side. Now, start the downswing by casting
your wrist. Can you see how this sends the club out and away from the
downward plane? It is also causing your arms to straighten out immediately
from the top. What is this doing to your relationship with the Father and
Son? It is forcing them away from you.

If this casting motion occurs, there isn't much hope for a good golf
shot. I do, however, have a few suggestions if you just discovered you are
a "caster" of the club. First, work hard on pulling those hands down from
the top, and feel your right elbow working close to your side. Second, I
want you to relax. This casting motion can occur many times because
people are very tense in starting their downswing. I think they feel like
they have to swing their arms very hard to hit the ball a long distance.

You already know that we are generating power by the club following the turn of our body as the Trinity works down the plane. So loosen up those arms, shoulders, and hands, and let them flow with your turn. Do you remember the idea behind your "soft?" The same reasoning applies here. If you stay relaxed, your body will respond the way it naturally wants to, and it will reduce your tendency to go fishing. If you do want to go fishing on the golf course, take your bait and pole to a lake and see if you can find the monster that got away. Just remember not to take the casting motion back to the golf course when you tee it up.

Falling Back:

While we are at it, let's learn from another common mistake I see in a lot of golfers I earlier classified as "dippers." These were the people who failed to transfer their weight to the right side at the top of their backswing. This lack of weight transfer resulted in a dipping of the left shoulder. So how do these dippers start their downswing? First you must ask where does their weight have to go in order to get the club through at impact? Does their lower body lead while the upper lags? Heck no! How can they transfer their weight into the ball when it is already on the left side? The resulting motion is a weight transfer over to the right side. These people are playing golf backwards. Have you ever seen the golfers that fall backwards off the ball as they hit it? This just does not make sense. As stated before, you need to transfer your weight to your right side before you can transfer it back through on the downswing.

I want to compare this idea of weight transfer to a few other athletic motions. First, let's look at a baseball pitcher. How does a pitcher complete his throwing motion? He starts his wind-up by turning his body to the top of the mound. He is transferring all of his weight to the right side by picking his left foot completely off the ground. After completing the wind-up, he begins his move to the plate by making an aggressive transfer of weight to his left foot. He releases the ball, and his right side then follows all the way through passing his left. He is moving in a positive direction when throwing to home plate. It would not make sense for him to throw the ball while falling backwards on top of the mound. He wouldn't have any velocity on the ball and very little control.

What about the batter? He starts his motion into the ball with his weight back on the right foot, which is just like the golf swing. He then strides forward with his left foot, planting it into the ground, and allowing the rest of his body to turn into the ball. Again, this is a positive motion. If he started with his weight on his left foot, he would start in a dipping position and have to shift his weight to the right side to get the bat through. These motions do not comply with the natural motions of the sport. The good thing is that you already know how to combat this dipping motion by allowing your upper body to travel to your right side as you complete the turn of your backswing.

From now on, if you see a buddy falling back on the downswing, explain to him why he is a dipper, and advise him to model the weight transfer of a baseball player. Once he gets the feel for the move and starts hitting the ball with more power and accuracy, he will be indebted to you for the rest of his golfing life. I only hope he is your partner come Saturday mornings.

Black Eye for Satan:

Well, well, well, Mr. Satan, what are you going to do now? Where are you going to run? Where are you going to hide? Was your desire to be greater than God worth it? Being created as the highest angel just wasn't good enough for you was it? You had to have it all. But you see, Satan, you forgot one important thing. How can you surpass the greatness of the One who created you? How can you dethrone the One who made the throne? How could you expect to be greater than the God who laid the foundations of the earth, determined its measurements, stretched the line upon it, fastened its foundation, and laid its cornerstone? (See **Job 38:4-6**.)

How could you expect to be greater than the God who shut in the sea with doors when it burst forth and issued from the womb; the God who made the clouds its garment, and thick darkness its swaddling band; and the God who fixed His limit for it, and set bars and doors when He said, *"This far you may come, but no farther, and here your proud waves must stop!"* (**Job 38:8-11**) No, Satan, you must not have been thinking very clearly on the day you left heaven to try and rule on your own.

It is time for you to face the reality of your fate. It is time to submit to the almighty, all-powerful, God. The seven years of the Tribulation are over. The Lord has allowed you to do enough damage. It is time for the second coming of the One who has all authority. You know every word of the Bible, Satan, but let me refresh your memory. *"Then I saw heaven opened, and behold, a white horse. And He who sat on him was called Faithful and True, and in righteousness He judges and makes war. His eyes were like a flame of fire, and on His head were many crowns. He had*

68

a name written that no one knew except Himself. He was clothed with a robe dipped in blood, and His name is called The Word of God. And the armies in heaven, clothed in fine linen, white and clean, followed Him on white horses. Now out of His mouth goes a sharp sword, that with it He should strike the nations. And He Himself will rule them with a rod of iron. He Himself treads the winepress of the fierceness and wrath of Almighty God. And He has on His robe and on His thigh a name written: KING OF KINGS AND LORD OF LORDS." (**Rev. 19:11-16**)

Yes, Satan, Jesus is coming back and it is time for you to leave. *"Then I saw an angel coming down from heaven, having the key to the bottomless pit and a great chain in his hand. He laid hold of the dragon, that serpent of old, who is the Devil and Satan, and bound him for a thousand years; and he cast him into the bottomless pit, and shut him up, and set a seal on him, so that he should deceive the nations no more till the thousand years were finished."* (**Rev. 20:1-3**)

I know that you will have a final revolt after the Millennium, but you know your ultimate fate after that, too. *"Now when the thousand years have expired, Satan will be released from his prison and will go out to deceive the nations which are in the four corners of the earth, Gog and Magog, to gather them together to battle, whose number is as the sand of the sea. They went up on the breadth of the earth and surrounded the camp of the saints and the beloved city. And fire came down from God out of heaven and devoured them. And the devil, who deceived them, was cast into the lake of fire and brimstone where the beast and the false prophet are. And they will be tormented forever and ever."* (**Rev. 20:7-10**)

You know, Satan, I sometimes wonder how God is going to cast you into the lake of fire. Will a stern look be enough to cause you to leap in yourself? How about an encouraging nudge? Personally, I am kind of hoping He reaches way back to the southern most tip of creation, clenches his fist, and lands a punch so firmly across your cheek that a black eye will be left for eternal remembrance. I think the Lord could muster enough force to land you at the bottom of the lake with a swift, right-cross. What would it feel like, Satan, for the fist of God to reach its impact on your face? I am thankful to never have to deal with you again after the Lord takes care of you like no one else can. Thank you, Jesus.

Wouldn't that be great to watch God T.K.O. Satan over the top rope into the lake of fire forever? I bet the angels and saints will be partying on that great day. It may be a while before we get to witness this event, but we do have an opportunity to do a little damage to Satan in the golf swing.

This, of course, would be at impact. This is the place where we get to release all of the force we have been storing, and cast Satan into the lake of fire for eternity.

Impact

From a mechanical perspective, I want to keep the move through impact pretty simple. The impact position should be a positive result from good preparation. The work we have done in the approach to impact has put us in a great position from which to strike the ball effectively. I now want to build upon this work in explaining where you need to be at impact.

First, let me talk about the turn of your body. This is very simple—the body keeps on turning. At this point, the idea of a continual body turn should be second nature to you. The turn of your body is a constant throughout the entire swing. My concern is that some of you are decreasing your body turn at impact because you are focusing on hitting the ball with your arms. Remember, the power in your golf swing comes from the turning of your big muscles as the smaller muscles in your arms follow. I would prefer you not to hit at the ball, but rather turn through it.

Second, I want to combine weight transfer with body position. The lead/lag relationship between the upper and lower body continues as more weight is being transferred to the left side. As we were building to the top of the backswing, our weight was accumulating on the right side and being absorbed in the right hip. At impact we will feel even more weight building up on the left side; particularly the left hip. I guess you could look at the transfer of weight in the golf swing as going from one hip to the other. This is the leading motion of the lower body in the lead/lag relationship. The lag is again reserved for the upper body.

The best visual image I can relate to you of the upper body lagging at impact is the picture of Ben Hogan on his company's equipment. It looks as if his head is two feet behind the ball. It probably is a good foot. If his head is staying behind the ball, wouldn't his upper body stay behind it too? When Hogan turns his weight to the left side, he is one of the best I have ever seen at keeping his upper body behind the ball at impact. I will soon explain why this is so important.

You can also see this very well in Kenny's position at impact. You can see how the weight in his lower body has transferred nicely to the left side, while the upper body has remained behind the ball.

Trinity Update:

Let's check in with the Trinity and see what they are doing at impact. This is a very happy time for the Trinity, because they get to use the club head as a means to deliver that eternal black eye Satan so greatly deserves. Mechanically, the Trinity is continuing to function in the same realm of connection. Do not lose sight of the connection the Trinity has to the turn of your body. The club is still following the turn of your body via the connection it has to the Holy Trinity.

Earlier, I related the idea of allowing the turn of your connected triangle to open the door on the way back. It is now time to close it by turning the triangle back through impact. At impact, you will find that the triangle has unfolded and straightened itself out. The elbows of the Father and Son are not bent but starting to extend. This is all part of unleashing the power in the club head. I think you will find it interesting that the Holy Spirit is slightly ahead of the ball and club head at impact. You will actually find that it is almost impossible to hit a good golf shot unless the hands are leading the club head at impact. This position of the Holy Spirit ahead of the club head at impact is a direct result of the pulling motion which helped initiate the downswing. So, if the hands are leading from the top, you should be in good shape at impact.

Through the hitting area:

We know that we are continuing our turn as we transfer more weight to the left side, the upper body continues to lag behind the lower, and the hands are ahead of the club head and ball at impact. What I need you to understand is, why! With respect to the transfer of weight, we have already covered this pretty well. (Nobody wants to be a dipper and fall backwards through impact.) The hands leading is another story. Let's start by considering what we are trying to accomplish. We know that the club is working on a plane toward the ball from the inside. We also know that we have to get that club face closing through impact or we are going to be in the trees on the right all day. How are we going to do this? Part of the answer lies in the turn itself.

If we are turning a connected triangle through impact, doesn't it make sense that the club face will be turning through as well? It should. The club face is actually turning around the ball at impact from inside out. This is what causes the ball to draw from right to left.

Now, let's investigate why the hands are ahead of the club head at impact. I just stated that the club face is turning around the ball at impact. Therefore, the club face is actually coming into the impact zone slightly open and closing to a square position for the split second the ball is on the surface of the club face. The club face works into the ball slightly open, which explains why the hands will be ahead of the ball and the club face at impact. The reality of this statement is that it is almost impossible to hit a good shot when your hands are not slightly ahead of the clubhead at impact. If your hands were in line with the club head, which is in line with the ball, the club face would be closing through the hitting area very quickly because it is traveling much faster than the hands. If the club face is closed and works through impact ahead of the hands, you are going to be in the trees on the left all day. You are also not going to make solid contact.

The best way for you to experience this is to try it yourself. Stop your swing and pose at the impact position. You may have never noticed it, but I bet your hands are ahead of the ball. In contrast, the next time you are hitting balls, make an effort to keep your hands behind the ball as the club head turns through ahead of them. Also, make sure there is nothing to your left you would want to hit. Again, if the club face is closing through impact ahead of the hands, the ball will most likely travel to the left.

Finally, I want to get back to Ben Hogan, the position of his upper body at impact, and why this is so crucial through the hitting area. First, wouldn't you agree that it is much easier to turn the club head through the ball if your upper body is lagging behind? It may only be a matter of two or three inches, but it is certainly enough room for your body and arms to turn the club through. You are giving yourself some security space. Now let's relate the path of the club to your upper body position at impact. Our goal from the top of the backswing is to allow the club to work on a plane that is down-and-out.

We have already taken care of the "down" part, but what about the "out?" The out, or **extension**, is directly related to your upper body staying behind the ball through the hitting area. If we are going to cast Satan into the lake of fire, we do not want to dribble him over the edge. We want to knock him all the way into the middle. We can do this by getting great extension of the club and arms through impact.

If your upper body lags behind, as Hogan's does, where do your arms have to go? They have to extend out, away from your body. This is extending the club head farther down the target line. You will also find your right forearm naturally turning over the left through the hitting area as the Trinity follows your body turn. This is a natural correlation to the turning of the club face around the ball. If your arms and club are extending far down the target line as your body continues its turn, what do you get? **POWER!**

74

A lot of great things happen when you allow the upper body to stay behind the ball at impact and through the hitting area. However, a lot of people have a difficult time translating this move from their brain to their body. Let me try and clear up some of the confusion.

When I am making this change in a student's swing, they will often over-exaggerate it. They turn a lagging upper body into an upper body that never gets in the car and falls way behind. The point I want to make here is that the upper body does move forward into the ball from the top of the backswing. The key is that it only moves so far forward. I want the upper body moving forward in a positive direction, but I want it to remain behind the ball at impact. By keeping your upper body way behind the ball, you are minimizing the turn of your upper body and not allowing the club head to turn through the ball. I see students who keep their upper body well behind the ball and have great extension, but the club face stays open, and the ball hangs on a string to the right. The upper-body position looks good, but you cannot forget to turn your right side back into the ball. A key I use when practicing is to feel like the "lat" muscles of my right side are turning aggressively into the ball as my head stays positioned behind it. So, do not be afraid to turn into the ball; just remember to look like Hogan once you get there.

Don't Get Jammed:

Do you ever feel like you are working hard to get the club through the ball, but your shots are still going off to the right? The harder you try, the farther to the right they go. Well, it is time to keep learning from our mistakes. Not everyone has the balance and upper-body positioning of Ben Hogan. You should be aware of how your upper body position at impact is affecting your shots. A very common fault found in almost every golfer's swing, including the pros at times, is an **upper body that leads ahead of the ball at impact.**

Remember, I want your upper body to turn into the ball to the point that it is not moving ahead of the ball. What happens if you turn past that point? When you turn your upper body ahead of the ball at impact, you **jam yourself**. I know you have all felt it, but let me explain what is happening.

You are working down into the ball, your upper body slides past the point of no return, and the club face is still working from the inside. Do you remember the security space I described when you stay behind the ball? Forget it, it's out the window. You have no comfort zone from which to turn the club face through the ball. Your body is in trouble, and it doesn't know what to do. If the club face doesn't start closing soon, you might miss the ball entirely.

Your body has one option, and it goes for it. Your brain decides your body needs more room to get the club through, and it commands the upper body to **lift up**. This lifting motion gives you enough room to quickly pull the club face back into the hitting area, and somehow make solid contact with the ball. You are essentially stopping the upper body from sliding too far ahead of the ball, and quickly turning an open club face into the ball with your right side. Is this a good thing? Not exactly.

Let's look at the path of the club resulting from this "lifting" motion. The club is initially working down the plane from a good angle. However, when you get jammed and your upper body lifts up, you are essentially pulling the club across the ball and the plane. You can see this in your divots. You will notice the divot starts out straight, but makes a strong turn to the left at the end. If you were a "**divotologist**," you could identify the point at which you got yourself jammed and had to pull the club face across the ball, inside the plane. Becoming a divotologist is good, because you learn a lot about the path of your club face at impact. If you understand the path of the divot, there is a good chance you will understand the flight of the ball. Once you have the mental understanding, you can transfer it into physical results. And this is a good thing.

How about extension? Do you have the extension you felt when your upper body stayed behind the ball? No, it is not even close. The lifting motion pulls your arms in close to your body, and they are not extending out in a straightened position. Your arms are actually forced to bend a little past the hitting area. You can count on losing 20 to 30 yards distance off the tee. Don't tell the golf ball manufacturers this, but the first step to getting more distance is not in the ball. It is in the upper-body position coupled with a good turn. Which one would you take, a longer ball or more powerful golf swing?

Here is another one for you. Where do you think the ball is going when you get jammed? How about to the right? Yes, this is the most probable result you can expect. The club face is still coming into the ball slightly open at impact. Yet, instead of turning around the ball from right to left, the face is pulled across the ball putting a left-to-right spin on the ball. The ball may start out on line, but the spin generates a fade or slice. This is the most frustrating result for me when playing or practicing. I would much rather play a draw than a fade. It is a more controllable ball for me, and I like the power. If you are struggling with "the fades," check your upper body at impact making sure you have not turned it too far forward into the "jam zone."

Remember to be patient with your upper body just as the Lord wants us to be patient with Him. I feel like my upper body gets greedy in my golf swing. It wants it all right now. It wants to know the future, where it will be, and what it will be doing. If my upper body were a human, it would not be satisfied with the reality of God's grace in its everyday situation. It would always be looking ahead to see the outcome before it happens. The only problem is that it will be looking to the right side of the golf course all day as a result of the fade it keeps producing. I know it is difficult, but I really think the Lord wants us to be patient with our upper body, stay behind the ball, and watch our ball find the desired target. Of course, He desires us to be patient with Him, let Him work through us, and know Him better. Jesus said, *"And this is eternal life, that they may know You, the only true God, and Jesus Christ whom You have sent"*. (**John 17:3**)

The Lord just wants us to know him better each day. He doesn't want us to be greedy like our upper bodies through impact. How about starting to be more patient and getting to know the Lord the way he wants us to? When we do this, He will extend the length of our fruitfulness like a 300-yard drive down the middle. Our strength will be renewed, and we will find eternal life in knowing Him.

Replaning the Club:

We have just looked at the necessity of keeping our upper body behind the ball at impact, and I want to touch on one more mechanical idea through the hitting area. This is the necessity of replaning the club after making contact with the ball. Remember, we need to have the club turning around the ball through impact, and this turning motion will continue as the Trinity Triangle remains connected to our body turn past impact.

From the Trinity's perspective, you will be feeling the Father staying close to your side as your club and arms extend through the hitting area. Try this for yourself. As you are swinging through the ball, make an effort to keep the Father, or left elbow, close to your side. Can you feel how this forces the club face to turn through the ball as your body continues to turn? This is really what it is all about. A lot of people try and turn the club face through by aggressively rolling their forearms and hands around the ball.

They allow their arms and hands to take over and break the bond of the Trinity with the body turn. So, remember to keep the Father close to your side as the club is turning through impact, and allow the body to turn the club around the ball. After all, keeping the Father close to your side can only be helpful.

Jesus Was Not A Quitter:

It is time to take it back home. Satan has been cast into the lake of fire forever, and Dad is ready for the joy of eternal life with all of His children. When we started the downswing and left the upper echelon of heaven, I promised that we would soon return. The unfinished business of destroying Satan has been completed, and heaven awaits us. From a mechanical view, all we have to do is finish the golf swing. We have established a strong position through impact, good extension, and tremendous power. So, the rest should be a piece of cake, right? Well, it will be if you remember one thing.

What have we used throughout the entire swing to guide the Trinity Triangle and club? Does the turning of our body sound familiar? So, what is it you need to remember to do? **Complete the swing by continuing the turn of your body.** I can be perfect from address to the top and back to impact, but if I stop my turn and neglect finishing the swing, mediocre play is about the best I can hope for. The final result I have worked so hard for will be unfulfilled, and I will be lost in a state of bewilderment. In the eyes of the golfing world, I will be seen as a quitter.

Do you feel like you just can't follow through on whatever it is you set out to do? It can be anything at all. I know I feel this way sometimes. Luckily, I have found the consequences are usually mild and not a matter of life and death. There is usually a second chance if we look hard enough. But what if Jesus had quit? What if He did not follow through with his mission? What if the Lord Jesus Christ reached the top of Calvary, was about to have the nails driven through his feet and hands, and he decided to quit? You know, he could have.

It would have been very easy for Him to have looked back on his life, seen all of the good he had done, and negotiated a deal with the Father. He could have said, "Hey Dad, wait a minute. Let's think about this a little more before we do something hasty here. I mean, come on, give me a little break on this one. I really don't deserve this treatment. After all, I have done an awful lot for these undeserving people as it is.

You know, Dad, I did leave your side in the kingdom to be born of flesh and blood on the earth. I lived in less-than-satisfactory conditions. I performed the manual labor of a carpenter, wearing out the skin of my hands. I taught Your word in the temple when I was just a boy. When You wanted me to leave my parents to tell the people of Your word, I did not hesitate. I have healed the sick. I have fed the hungry. I have given sight to the blind. I have allowed the lame to walk again. I have returned sound to the ears of the deaf. I have calmed the wind, sea, and rain to prove Your power. I did not give in to one of Satan's temptations. I have shown true love to every person I have come into contact with. I have formed a group of apostles, and they are going to continue spreading the word to the whole world. So, Dad, what do you say? Why don't we just skip this dying part and let me join you back in heaven right now? I miss you Dad, and I would really like to come home."

I think if Jesus had pleaded with the Father long enough, he could have skipped this one minor event. He could have called on a band of angels to fly down, take him off the cross, and escort him back to the loving arms of the Father. With the snap of a finger, they would have obeyed his every command. He could have stopped the journey right there and not followed through with his entire purpose of coming to the Earth. It would have been a lot easier for Him, wouldn't it? **But, He didn't!** Jesus said in **John 6:38** *"For I have come down from heaven, not to do My own will, but the will of Him who sent Me."* This is what I want you to think about when it comes time to finish your golf swing. Jesus was not a quitter, and neither are you.

In concluding the swing, there are only a few things I want you to remember. First, you have to continue turning all the way to the top. After all, we do want to get back to heaven, don't we? To do this, we have to get the Holy Trinity back to the upper echelon reached at the top of the backswing. Look at it from the perspective of not completing your turn. Where do your hips and shoulders point if you stop turning? They point to the right of your target. Will the club replane if the turn stops? Where is the ball most likely going to wind up if your hips and shoulders are pointed to the right and the club never replanes? Yes, out to the right as well. Are you familiar with the term **deceleration**? This is exactly what you are doing by not continuing your turn all the way to the top. When you decelerate and stop the club short of heaven, you are losing a lot of power and control over the shot. So utilize the tool of turning your body to its fullest extent, and keep turning all the way to the top.

Finally, there needs to be a complete transfer of weight to the left side. It is time to let your upper body catch up to the lower as you come to a rest in your follow through. I don't want you to be afraid to let your right foot come up on its toe as your weight is transferred to the left side. If you are going to turn your body all the way through, it helps to bring the weight up off the right foot.

While holding his finish, you can see how well Kenny has turned through and transferred his weight. He is well balanced on his left side, and his hips and shoulders are pointing squarely to his target. Notice how nice and high he holds his finish. Once you start hitting good shots like Kenny, you too will hold your finish high and long as you admire the flight of the ball at your target.

Well, the vision has been completed. You are standing tall, holding a beautiful finish as you watch a towering drive land in the middle of the fairway. The club is back in the upper echelon of heaven, returning the Holy Trinity to its rightful place. It is good to be back home. Congratulations on finishing the golf swing in beautiful form and enjoying the Lord in heaven. It's OK, you can smile if you want to. After hitting a great shot and posing at the top in heaven, you deserve to smile. Just remember to tell the others in your foursome the reason for your smile: **Jesus**.

Mechanical Summary:
God's Grace Is The Answer

In looking back at the mechanical details described in this book, I realize there are more than a few thoughts to comprehend. I know that physical changes are not easy to make, but I encourage you to work on them and to be patient. The results will just take a little time.

From a more comforting point of view, I want to encourage you to have a spiritual outing while playing golf. I mentioned at the beginning of the section on the full swing that I wanted to keep our thoughts as simple as possible. Let me share with you the way I play golf.

When I approach the ball from behind, I set my feet in the proper alignment knowing that I am stepping in the solid foundation of Christ. I then acknowledge the Trinity Triangle and give thanks to them for being in my golf swing. After this, I check the pressure of my soft by letting go of the world and trusting the Lord. Finally, I turn my body to the top of my backswing and back through to my finish position.

It has taken many hours of hard work on the driving range to get to this point, but this is how simple I keep my game on the course. It is quite spiritually fulfilling. Kenny and I have some of our best times on the golf course by having a little church while we play. We play better, and most importantly, we come to know the Lord a little better.

Throughout the entire mechanical sections of the book, I have drilled one idea into your head: The body turn directs the path of the club due to the connection of the Trinity Triangle. It is the body turn which allows all of this to happen. There is only one thing in my life that I can think of to relate to the simplicity of the body turn: **God's grace**. Just as God's grace allows everything to happen in my life, it is the body turn that allows the swing to work properly. This is it! God's grace oversees the entire workings of the golf swing in the form of body turn. Well then, I hope God's grace completely covers you every time you pick up a club. Praise to God!

Closing Thoughts: Jesus Loves You

Do you ever wonder why Jesus didn't just command the angels to save him from the pain of the cross and suffering through the agony of hell? Again, he could have done it very easily. I think the answer is very simple. Jesus stayed on the cross and died because he loves you. He has a longing so deep in his heart for your life that he allowed himself to be brutally crucified. The thought of losing you to the devil and a life in hell forever burdened Jesus so much that he gave all that he had for you. To me, Jesus dying on the cross is the biggest 'I Love You' card Hallmark could ever come up with. The main difference is that His words are written in red. His heart's cry is for you to know him as Lord and Savior so you can experience his love for eternity.

If you are not sure where you stand with the Lord and your eternal destination, please make the effort to be sure. Before you put this book on the shelf to start collecting dust, contact a Christian friend, a church leader, or someone who can help answer any questions you might have. In the end, it doesn't matter who we are, what we do, or what we have. Our Salvation is the only thing that matters. I recently saw a sign from the American Lung Association that read, "If you aren't breathing, nothing else matters". I don't mean any disrespect to the ALA, but I disagree. If you aren't breathing, the only thing that matters is whether or not you know Jesus as Lord and Savior. Don't wait until the end of your life to worry about your eternal future. After all, do any of us know when the end of the road will come?

I once heard a friend say, "I know more golf than I am playing." He knew how to play better golf but just could not get his body to respond the way he wanted it to. Do any of you know more about Christianity than you are living? I know I do. If we know how to better live our lives for the Lord, why aren't we doing it? I guess this is my revival statement for all of us. I know we can all do a little more to make a difference for God's kingdom. So I encourage those of you who are sure of your eternal destination to do a little more to ensure someone around you has a ticket of admission into heaven with you. If someone had not shared with you, wouldn't you hate to be left behind?

Please know that I have thoroughly enjoyed sharing my knowledge of golf mechanics and who I am with you. I encourage you to work hard on the changes you will make, and do not be frustrated if the results are not immediate. It takes time for the muscles to adapt to what your mind is saying to them.

I also hope I have been able to comfortably relate to you the joy that the Lord brings to me through golf and the love that he has for you. I pray you will allow Him to work in your life for His glory. May God bless you.

Down the Middle,

Hammett-up!!

About the Author

Chuck Hammett was born December 29, 1968, and grew up in Venice, Florida. He is the son of Richard and Lynn Hammett, with one brother, Trey. The Hammett family has resided in Venice since the early 1960's. The game of golf was introduced to Chuck at the early age of seven by his father. Many other sports also occupied Chuck's time from an early age, having been blessed with natural atheletic ability. Thanks to a strong junior golf asociation in nearby Sarasota, the desire to compete came about naturally. It became evident that Chuck would excel in golf by his mid-teens, and all the other sports soon took a back seat to his focus on golf.

After graduating from Venice High School in 1987, Chuck accepted a golf scholarship to Stetson University, where he graduated in 1991. While at Stetson, Chuck graduated with a bachelors of science in chemistry with honors. He was looking to go to medical school. Chuck was lured to Tallahassee, Florida in October of 1991 while waiting to be accepted to medical school. Fortunately, no acceptance letters were received and a change of direction was necessary. It was during this time that he began attending the First Baptist Church of Tallahassee, and sought to develop a stronger relationship with the Lord.

It was evident to Chuck that he was blessed with the ability to teach, and spent two years as the director of science at Shepherd Academy in Tallahassee. However, his passion for the game of golf was ever present, and he began looking for opportunities to teach. Chuck was taken on as an instructor in the Bill Skelley School of Golf in 1992.

In February of 1993, Chuck felt a strong call from the Lord to write a book for Him. Out of that call has come this book, "Jesus Would Have Been A Scratch Golfer", and Fore Him Ministries of which Chuck is director. It was not until the latter part of 1993 that Chuck started his friendship with Kenny and Karen Knox. It was out of their strong desire for ministry that led Kenny to become involved in Chuck's ministry. This friendship has also led to Chuck becoming one of the head instructors at the Kenny Knox Golf Academy in Tallahassee where he is currently teaching full time.

While teaching golf is the medium for Chuck's ministry, sharing the gospel of Jesus Christ is the burden of his heart. Chuck has been speaking in churches, sharing the Lord's message in this most unique manner, since June of 1994. He has also appeared on the Christian radio networks. Chuck's ministry seeks to present the message of Christ in a way people can comfortably relate to, and challenge them in ways never thought of before.

Speaking engagements with this dynamic speaker can be arranged by contacting Chuck, c/o Fore Him Ministries, P.O. Box 11073, Tallahassee, Florida 32302-3073, or at (904) 222-3611. This a one of a kind presentation you won't want to miss.

NOTES

NOTES

NOTES

NOTES

NOTES